More praise fo

'Eminently readable, intensely practical and deeply insightful. Charting the journey of the first year of loss as Tony does is so very helpful to those who are living through that experience. My own wife, Barbara, died in 2016, and as I read *Grief Notes* I couldn't help thinking this book would have been an invaluable gift to me during my own first year of grieving.'

Revd Ian Jennings, Anglican priest and author of *By a Departing Light*

'Many books are written for those grieving or supporting the bereaved, but *Grief Notes* is particularly valuable as a brave, raw, inspiring and practical account of Tony's first year without Evelyn, a grief journey that is unique and without end.'

Ro Willoughby, lay minister, writer and fellow traveller in grief

'This book is so honest, raw and painful to read at times (as it echoes a similar journey my father is on), but Tony still shares with such clarity and wisdom even in the midst of his own personal grief.'

Claire Musters, writer, speaker and editor

'Tony brings insight and wisdom to the subject of bereavement from his personal experience. This book is both thought-provoking and helpful, even seven years after my own wife's death.'

Roger Womack, grief support volunteer and founder of LossandLife.org

15 The Chambers, Vineyard
Abingdon OX14 3FE
brf.org.uk

Bible Reading Fellowship (BRF) is a charity (233280)
and company limited by guarantee (301324),
registered in England and Wales

ISBN 978 1 80039 126 0
First published 2022
10 9 8 7 6 5 4 3 2 1 0
All rights reserved

Text © Tony Horsfall 2022
This edition © Bible Reading Fellowship 2022
Cover artwork © Martin Beek, after a photograph by David Tanner

Acknowledgements

Unless otherwise stated, scripture quotations are taken from The Holy Bible, New International Version (Anglicised edition) copyright © 1979, 1984, 2011 by Biblica. Used by permission of Hodder & Stoughton Publishers, an Hachette UK company. All rights reserved. 'NIV' is a registered trademark of Biblica. UK trademark number 1448790.

Scripture quotation on p. 44 is from The Amplified Bible (AMP), copyright 2015 by The Lockman Foundation. Used by permission. lockman.org

Scripture quotation marked KJV is taken from The Authorised Version of the Bible (The King James Bible), the rights in which are vested in the Crown, reproduced by permission of the Crown's Patentee, Cambridge University Press.

Scripture quotation from *The Message* is copyright © 1993, 1994, 1995, 1996, 2000, 2001, 2002 by Eugene H. Peterson. Used by permission of NavPress. All rights reserved. Represented by Tyndale House Publishers, Inc.

A catalogue record for this book is available from the British Library

Printed by CPI Group (UK) Ltd, Croydon CR0 4YY

Grief Notes
Walking through loss
The first year after bereavement

Tony Horsfall

*To all who grieve, in whatever way –
may you know God's comfort
and find strength for every day.*

*And those who help others who grieve –
may you know God's wisdom and compassion
as you accompany them.*

Photocopying for churches

Please report to CLA Church Licence any photocopy you make from this publication. Your church administrator or secretary will know who manages your CLA Church Licence.

The information you need to provide to your CLA Church Licence administrator is as follows:

Title, Author, Publisher and ISBN

If your church doesn't hold a CLA Church Licence, information about obtaining one can be found at **uk.ccli.com**

Contents

Foreword 7

Introduction 9

July 2020 | Responding 13

August 2020 | Adjusting 22

September 2020 | Stabilising 31

October 2020 | Learning 41

November 2020 | Understanding 51

December 2020 | Accepting 61

January 2021 | Descending 73

February 2021 | Struggling 87

March 2021 | Re-emerging 100

April 2021 | Reconnecting 112

May 2021 | Re-envisioning 125

June 2021 | Repositioning 137

July 2021 | Reflecting 146

Epilogue 154

Notes 156

Further reading 158

Helpful resources and courses 160

Foreword

I first met Tony Horsfall when we were both students at London Bible College. We played on the college football and rugby teams together, and I was always impressed with Tony's friendliness and consistency. What you saw was what you got. He was a man of integrity and never afraid to express his opinion, and that straightforward approach made him many friends.

I graduated a year ahead of Tony and moved to Canada to marry my wife, Carolyn. Over the next 40-plus years, Tony and I didn't have regular contact, although I would hear about him and his ministry from fellow students.

God has a wonderful way of bringing people back into your life when the time is right. Tony and I reconnected, and he came to a seminar I was conducting not far from his home. The friendship was reignited, and it has been my privilege to 'draw near' and walk alongside Tony through the final days of dear Evelyn's illness and then through his grief journey after she died.

Tony has not changed much in the near 50 years since we were students together. What you see is still what you get. He is, maybe even more, a person of integrity and a man of God. I am very moved by the honesty, vulnerability and insight he brings to this book. But that's Tony Horsfall.

In this touching and inspiring book, he shares from his heart as a 'wounded healer', making his own wounds a gift for those who hurt. You will find that his words will validate the many emotions of grief, which many people are afraid to express lest they be thought of as 'weak'. Believe me, it takes someone of strength and authenticity to say, 'I'm hurt, but I am healing.'

May everyone who reads this book find encouragement to know that God cares about us, even in our brokenness, and promises to 'draw near and walk alongside'. May you feel the presence of the Lord Jesus, the 'man of sorrows', who was 'acquainted with grief' and has promised to be 'with us'.

Thank you, Tony, for sharing from your heart and for allowing me the privilege of being a companion on your journey.

Dr Bill Webster, executive director, The Centre for the Grief Journey

Introduction

Grief did not begin for me on the day my wife Evelyn died. It started four years earlier in 2016, when we received the diagnosis that, after an absence of five years, breast cancer had returned and was 'not curable, but containable'. Yes, treatment was available, but it would not take away the cancer, only delay the inevitable.

Of course, we believed that God could heal her. We received much prayer and sought opportunities to be prayed for, often with the anointing of oil. There were special experiences of God's nearness, like when we prayed together in the church on Holy Island, and Evelyn – not given to emotional display – began to shake with the sense of God's presence. But we remained realistic too. Perhaps the four years we had together after the diagnosis were a gift, the answer to our prayers. Maybe our prayers were only delaying the inevitable, but they gave us precious time.

The first round of treatment for Evelyn was horrendous. She not only experienced the usual loss of hair, sickness and fatigue, but frequent nose bleeds and the need for blood transfusions. A change to tablets was easier to deal with but made no impression on the cancer. Then she was given a third drug, again by infusion. More hair loss followed, as well as blackened fingernails and toenails, and this time painful lymphoedema in her left arm. How much she suffered, but always bravely and without self-pity or complaint.

All the while our world was becoming smaller – restricted and uncertain. It was hard to plan anything, and we grew increasingly limited in what we could do. It was like watching a row of dominos collapse, one piece hitting another until none were left standing. Grief had already taken hold in me as I watched her suffer and her world shrink before my eyes.

For years our routine was to go out on Saturdays for coffee and shopping. We enjoyed various locations on a sort of rota basis, but our most frequent haunt was Meadowhall, a large shopping centre on the edge of Sheffield. Normally we would get there early, then go our separate ways for an hour or so, before meeting up for coffee and to read the newspaper. It was a happy, relaxing routine we both enjoyed.

Gradually, though, even this little tradition became harder to maintain. Evelyn could not walk as far, so we reduced our shopping time. Occasionally she would hire a mobile scooter from the shopping centre or take her tripod with wheels to help her walk. Eventually when that became too much, we were reduced to a quick half-hour visit for a coffee using a wheelchair, then back home. In the end we could no longer make trips like this at all. The domino effect was at work.

When the cancer spread into her spine at the start of 2020, we entered another stage of loss. Hope of a cure was now gone and being nursed at home soon became impossible, even though we tried. Evelyn's ability to care for herself was decreasing rapidly, and she was losing her independence. This increased as we went together into the local hospice, and then a care home. I had decided to accompany Evelyn, because visiting was not allowed during the pandemic, and the thought of being separated was too much to bear. Over the weeks she became immobile, needed a hoist to get in and out of bed and lost control of her bodily functions. Watching all this was hard, and tears flowed freely. My grief journey was well underway.

Evelyn eventually died on 13 July 2020. I use the word 'died' deliberately, for that is the hard reality, and it cannot be softened by saying she 'passed away' or, even more inanely, 'she passed'. Nor do I like to say I 'lost' her, because I didn't lose her. No, she died, but not in a way that meant it was the end. She died with the confident expectation of life in heaven, of entering into the presence of the God she had loved and served all her life. That strong belief tempers my sense of loss. She is most definitely in a better place, free of suffering and pain, at home with her Lord.

It is we who are left to grieve her death who may have some hard days ahead of us. It is uncharted territory, and we do not know what challenges we may face. We do know, though, that God will not leave us nor forsake us, but will accompany us every step of the way on the journey of grief. I will not walk this road alone, and I invite you to walk with me in the hope that my experience will be an encouragement to you should you ever walk this path yourself.

Perhaps at this point I should explain that what I have written is based on the notes I kept and the postings I made online during the first year of my bereavement. To this I have added insights I gained from scripture along the way, and from my readings around the subject of grief. I have been greatly helped on my journey by regular conversations with two good friends – Bill Webster, a hugely experienced grief counsellor based in Canada, and Debbie Hawker, a psychologist and member care specialist here in England. Bill has kindly given me permission to quote freely from, and paraphrase, his written materials, for which I am profoundly grateful.

This first year of my bereavement – July 2020 to July 2021 – took place during the coronavirus pandemic in the UK. It was thus lived out under heavy restrictions and months of harsh lockdown, which of course had a major impact on the shape of my grief journey, as it did for thousands of others. Everything was intensified and nothing was normal. The usual support systems were no longer there. But by the grace of God, and with the help of many amazing friends, I managed to come through, although sometimes it was touch and go.

It is my prayer that this combination of real-time personal experience, the wisdom of scripture and the insights of grief counselling will be a help to others who are called to walk this path that no one chooses to take. Writing *Grief Notes* has certainly been a helpful form of therapy for me, and I trust it will strengthen you also. I am not a grief expert, and everyone's grief is expressed differently, so your path will not be the same as mine. Do not compare yourself to me. Yet there may be similarities, and there may be insights that will help you. Sometimes it is helpful simply to know that others have walked this way before.

JULY 2020

Responding

13 July

Evelyn passed away peacefully in the early hours of this morning. I had prayed with her last night before I left Cherry Trees, the care home where she was being nursed. Although at that stage she was not able to communicate much, at the end of my prayer she blurted out, 'Thank you, Jesus, you led me all the way.' These were the last words she spoke, and they gave me great assurance that she was ready to go home to be with Jesus. The home called me just after 2.00 am, but when I got there, she was gone. It was hard to see her lying there, lifeless, her skin cold and the colour of bone china. Even though expected, her death was still a shock. I packed her things and tidied her room as I waited for the undertaker to arrive. I spoke to my son Alistair in Australia, as I knew he would be awake. Then, with great dignity, she was taken away, and I was alone. I will never see her again on this earth.

A time for everything

You may be familiar with the great passage in Ecclesiastes 3:1–11 with its 14 statements about life, realities that are as true now as when they were when first written centuries before Christ was born. It begins like this: 'There is a time for everything, and a season for every activity under the heavens' (v. 1). Then comes the first punchline, describing the most universal of life experience, and it hits you hard in the stomach – 'a time to be born and a time to die' (v. 2). In a culture that likes to pretend that death is not real and can be avoided, we are pierced by the raw reality that there will come a moment in time when death touches every one of us.

Death is inevitable. There is a time to be born. There is a time to die. No one lives forever, and sooner or later we will become familiar with the reality that we – and those we love – are frail, finite creatures with a limited timespan on planet earth. We can celebrate births and birthdays with joy and gladness, but inevitably we shall also mourn the death of loved ones and grieve their passing with tears of sadness.

Grieving is painful, for as we read here there is also a time to weep (v. 4). Of course, we would prefer life to be all sunshine, every day filled with fun and laughter, but the shadow of death is never far away, especially as we get older. Grief is the price we pay for loving, and our tears reflect the pain we feel when we lose someone dear to us.

Grief is not permanent, however. We may never completely get over it, but we do come through it. There is 'a time to mourn and a time to dance' (v. 4). It may seem impossible when we are in the midst of grief to think that we could ever be happy again, but we will be. Slowly, with the passing of time and the brave work that grieving well requires of us, we will emerge into the brightness of a new day. Joy will return. That has to be our hope, for without such a prospect we may well stay submerged in the darkness of loss forever.

This truth gives us belief that we can find a way through our grief and come out the other side to live again. Yes, even to dance once more!

Understanding grief

According to Bill Webster, grief is 'the normal but bewildering cluster of ordinary human emotions arising in response to a significant loss, intensified and complicated by the relationship we have lost.'[1]

Within that cluster of emotions, we may find shock, numbness, confusion, lack of concentration, anxiety, panic, anger, guilt, fatigue, sadness and yearning. No two individuals experience grief in the same way. We all have our own unique cluster because we are all different people, and our relationships are different. Each person's response is different because of the many factors that make up the background to the loss.

In considering our loss we must ask about the relationship, 'What did this person give to me? What did the relationship mean to me? How will my life be different without them? What have I lost?' The death of someone we care about hurts very much. It affects us emotionally, physically, mentally and spiritually. The loss of a spouse is one of the most difficult experiences we ever face.

---

15 July

Today has been busy making practical arrangements. It helps to have something concrete to do, although in this time of pandemic, nothing is straightforward. The new government scheme 'Tell Us Once' is really helpful as the information about a death is passed on to those who need to know. There have been lots of phone calls to make as well, informing other people. They have already been to remove the hospital bed we had at home when we looked after her here, and also the wheelchair with which we made many visits to the hospital.

17 July

Friends called round to see me today; we can meet outside if socially distanced. It was Alan's birthday. How strange to sign his card with just my name. That's a first, and a gentle reminder that things are different.

If you ask me how I feel right now, I will say two words – relief and release. Relief that Evelyn is suffering no more; release that the responsibility of caring for her has been lifted from me. Those are not comfortable emotions, but that honestly is how it feels right now.

18 July

I phoned some of Evelyn's friends from her nursing days in Scotland, and they appreciated hearing from me. I cried as they told me stories of her life before I knew her. Who would have thought that she failed her nursing exams the first time because of too much socialising? She never told me that!

21 July

As Evelyn's health deteriorated, Jenny used to help us once a week with housework, but for family reasons had to stop. Now things are sorted at home she can come again and is delighted to help me. Today is her first day back. I am so relieved and see this as a provision of God. It will help me such a lot as I start rebuilding my life. These small things really matter. Evelyn and I had clear responsibilities when it came to the home. I did the finances, cut the grass, tried my hand at odd jobs (usually without success), but housekeeping was her domain. Cooking, washing, cleaning, gardening – these responsibilities she revelled in, and did well. What will I do without her? There is so much that I don't know, so many things that bewilder me. It feels like a mountain to climb. One step at a time then.

22 July

In my spare moments I have been trawling through our photo albums to select some suitable pictures to use in my tribute to Evelyn which I will share at a Zoom thanksgiving on Saturday. Needless to say, the tears have flowed freely as I have been reminded of her as a girl and teenager, then wife and mother. What a smile! No wonder I fell in love with her, and as I see her again in the years of our courtship and early marriage I am smitten once more. I remember at the time being challenged by some words supposedly from the great missionary Hudson Taylor: 'God gives his best to those who leave the choice to him.' He certainly gave me the best when he gave me Evelyn. We fitted together so well, like a hand in a glove.

25 July

This afternoon we held a thanksgiving service for Evelyn's life via Zoom, which meant that people all over the world could tune in. We had some serious technical difficulties to begin with, but got there in the end, and it was so comforting to hear different people from various stages of our life share their appreciation for Ev (as I call her). There are so many unusual aspects of grieving during a pandemic, so being able to experience this has been a bonus. Under normal circumstances we might not have thought of this way of connecting with friends in far-off places like Malaysia, where we lived for many years early in our marriage.

27 July

Tomorrow is the funeral, and I'm nervous about it. How will I feel when I see the coffin? What will my response be when it is lowered into the ground and covered with soil? These are unusual times for mourning. It will be in the open air at the graveside, so we are not limited for numbers, but there will be no singing, no hugging and no get together afterwards. Will people come, given the fear of contracting the virus? It seems strange that the grave is less than 200 yards from where we lived in Brierley for most of our married life. And in the same cemetery are the graves of my parents and my sister and her husband.

---

28 July

A wet and blustery day, but dry enough for the funeral at 1.00 pm. About 70 gathered, and it was a great service, ably led by our pastor, Ashley Guest. He knew Evelyn well and gave a moving tribute. Again, it was good to see people whom we had known over the years, including some of her work colleagues. I felt surprisingly calm throughout, perhaps even a bit numb, almost like a bystander. I so wanted to hug people, and to be hugged in return! A few family members came back to the house afterwards, but that was all. I wondered how I would feel when everyone had left and I was left alone, but I was fine. I know for some this moment is very difficult, but I got through it alright.

I am not at all superstitious, but during the service a white feather floated down from the sky, hovered around and, despite the blustery conditions, found its way right into the grave. Our daughter Debbie noticed it too. I don't know if it means anything, but it seemed unusual.

---

30 July

Having been together for 46 years, it seems so strange to be without Ev. I am happy enough in the house without her, having already had a month here by myself when I was recovering from the coronavirus. Seeing each day the chair where she normally sat has not phased me either, but deep inside I feel like something is missing. It is as if I have lost an arm and a leg. Part of me is gone; it is so strange. Last night I tiptoed to the toilet for fear of waking her. Today it seems like she is still in the care home and will come home soon. None of it is rational, but it is how it feels.

31 July
It has to be done. Evelyn's possessions have to be sorted out. The first stage has been alright, getting rid of old shoes and clothes she didn't wear. I've tidied up the bedroom she was using during her illness and got rid of a lot of papers that are not important. I've also returned surplus medicines to the chemist. But I will leave it there for now and leave the rest for another day. It is too painful to continue.

To die is gain

> For to me, to live is Christ and to die is gain. If I am to go on living in the body, this will mean fruitful labour for me. Yet what shall I choose? I do not know! I am torn between the two: I desire to depart and be with Christ, which is better by far; but it is more necessary for you that I remain in the body.
> PHILIPPIANS 1:21–24

The apostle Paul felt squeezed between life and death. On the one hand he might be put to death for his faith, which would mean entrance into the presence of Christ. He saw this as a glorious prospect. On the other hand, there was still work for him to do and he felt the responsibility to finish the task before him. This dilemma leads him to say, 'For to me, to live is Christ and to die is gain' (v. 21).

This scripture brought amazing comfort to both Evelyn and I as we contemplated her death. Since being a young girl growing up in Inverness, in the highlands of Scotland, her life was given to Christ. She dreamed of becoming a missionary nurse and prepared herself for that calling by training well. As it happened, she didn't do the nursing part overseas, but she did become a missionary; after we met at London Bible College, we served together in Malaysia, on the island of Borneo. There, for eight exciting years, we helped the emerging churches, packed with young people, to become established. Then, when we returned home in 1983, she partnered with me in pastoring a church in West Yorkshire. Later, she would return to nursing, eventually working with elderly mentally ill patients. Her greatest achievement was to help in the opening of a purpose-built Christian nursing home and to be the first matron. As a wife and mother, friend and colleague, she reflected the likeness of Christ and sought to serve him according to her gifts.

Now the second part of Paul's statement is true. She is in heaven with her Saviour, free of suffering and pain, and rejoicing in the glory that surrounds her. We miss her, but how could we deny her such a blessing? Knowing this certainly softens the blow of separation and moderates the pain of our loss.

Death is not the end, but a new beginning. For those with faith in Christ it brings the promise of heaven and ultimate healing. This is the lens through which we understand her dying, and this certainty can be yours as well.

Grief and mourning

Grief and mourning are common terms to describe feelings and behaviours following a loss. Although sometimes used interchangeably, grief and mourning represent different parts of loss. While grief describes the thoughts and feelings experienced following a loss, mourning covers the outward expressions or signs of grieving. Grief is internal; mourning is external.

Grief includes an acute phase, which happens shortly after a loss is experienced. Symptoms of acute grief can include sadness, heartache, confusion, longing to be with the deceased, intense thoughts and memories of the person, anxiety, guilt and anger. These feelings and thoughts are a normal reaction to losing someone. Often there will be a difference in how men and women express their grief, with women tending to be more expressive of emotion than men, who may deem crying to be a sign of weakness. National characteristics also play a part. British people, for example, like to keep a stiff upper lip and maintain their dignity. Other cultures are the exact opposite and may encourage weeping and wailing as a normal expression of grief.

While grief refers to the internal experiences of loss, mourning is best defined as acts or outward expressions of grief. Some common examples of mourning can include things like funeral customs, associated rituals, appropriate dress code, the way emotions are expressed, sharing memories or stories about a loved one, the length of time given to mourning and so on. These aspects of the mourning process are also hugely impacted by cultural norms and values, which themselves give structure to the grieving process.

Grief can mean different things for different people and there is no right or wrong way to grieve. Over time, grief typically decreases and may become more of a background feeling rather than a dominant, continual one.

AUGUST 2020

Adjusting

Comfort from God

> Praise be to the God and Father of our Lord Jesus Christ, the Father of compassion and the God of all comfort, who comforts us in all our troubles, so that we can comfort those in any trouble with the comfort we ourselves receive from God.
> 2 CORINTHIANS 1:3–4

When we lose a person who was dear to us, what we need above all is to be comforted. We need to feel safe, to feel understood, to know that everything will be alright. We are hurting, we feel wounded and we are in pain. We need reassurance.

Faith in God can make a huge difference to our ability to cope in this wounded state. For some, the anger that is a normal part of the grieving process at the injustice of it all is often directed towards God, and for a while faith may seem like a hindrance rather than a help. For others, though, a living faith can be a source of great comfort and solace as they look to God for daily strength and feel themselves upheld by the prayers of others.

In his own time of anguish and hurt, the apostle Paul turned to God for help, knowing him to be a Father who cares and is responsive to our cries for help. What we think about God really matters, for it determines how we will respond to him in a crisis. Here we learn that God is a Father who is compassionate towards us and shares our pains. He understands how we feel, knows the emotions we experience and is able to comfort us.

How does he do this? First, by speaking to us through the Bible, reminding us of the promises he has given to us, reassuring us that death is not the end.

Then, through the comforting words and presence of our friends – in their practical acts of kindness; in their cards, phone calls and messages; in their offering a listening ear or simply providing a reassuring presence. God is present in all these ways, and they are a great help.

But supremely his comfort comes in that mysterious sense of his presence with us – the ministry of the Holy Spirit when no one else is there, confirming we are not alone and bringing peace to our hearts. It is not really explainable or even describable, but it is real. He comes to us through the locked doors of our grief like the risen Jesus to his disciples, and he says, 'Peace be with you!' (John 20:19).

Grief is normal

'Grief is not a disease,' writes Dr Bill Webster. 'It is the normal human response to a significant loss.'[2] It is natural to feel upset, to shed some tears. This shows that you miss the person and are struggling to adapt to life without them. Such loss is a very personal matter, and your grief is painful. Although we may want to avoid the pain and have done with it as quickly as possible, we must be brave enough to go through the experience of grief and face up to our loss. The pain we feel will be in direct proportion to what has been lost from your life.

Grieving is like a journey, and dealing with it is sometimes called grief work because it requires effort on our part. This can be emotionally and physically draining. Many people will want us to get over our grief as quickly as possible so we can 'move on', but it is better to let grief takes its course. The first months may be the most intense. Usually, grief will come and go in waves and often takes longer than people think before it subsides. It is quite unpredictable, and in unexpected moments we may find ourselves acutely missing the person again. It can feel like a roller coaster – one minute we feel fine; the next we are in the depths of despair.

The death of a loved one is our main loss, but we will discover other associated losses (often referred to as secondary losses) as we realise how much we will miss not only the person but the many ways they contributed to our life. We find ourselves being impacted unexpectedly as things we once took for granted – for example, doing the cooking or paying the bills – no longer happen. Effective grief work is not done alone, and to get through we will need the help of family and friends, even occasionally a counsellor or specialist helper.

---

3 August
The 'Eat Out to Help Out' scheme, which was started to help the economy during the pandemic, means that restaurants and cafes are offering meals at reduced prices, subsidised by the government. This evening I have been to a local restaurant with my daughter Debbie and her family. It is such a joy to be with them and to have a nice meal together, but there is a pang of guilt that I can enjoy such a treat and Evelyn cannot.

---

4 August
Today is our 47th wedding anniversary. That's a long time to have

*been married to someone, and we shared so much together. We had
become so in tune with each other over the years, accepting both
our strengths and weaknesses. Grief, I know, is a very personal thing
and depends a lot on the depth of relationship you had with the one
you have lost. One thing that has helped me is that we had plenty
of time to plan ahead, and to talk through important matters. I
don't think there was anything left unsaid between us. I had the
opportunity to care for her during the months of her treatment, and
then to be with her in the care home for almost eight weeks. When
someone dies suddenly there is no such opportunity, and I can only
imagine how hard that must be.*

7 August

*I have made a little display for Evelyn in the living room. Not an
altar or shrine, but a simple arrangement of a photo of the two of
us, and one of the whole family, plus a nice plant and two of her
favourite brooches. It helps us to remember her – not that we are
likely to forget, but it is a way to say she is still part of this house.*

10 August

*I think today I experienced what is sometimes called a 'grief
ambush', a moment when we are suddenly aware of the reality of
our loss. I was doing the dishes at the sink and started to wash a
marmalade jar that was now empty. At the same moment I realised
with a jolt that this was the last jar of the marmalade that Evelyn
had made, and tears filled my eyes. Over many years she had made
her own marmalade, which we both enjoyed at breakfast. Now there
will be no more. A sudden realisation of loss, of what it will mean to
be without her. No more delicious marmalade.*

12 August

*In losing Evelyn a huge chunk of my life has gone, like when there is
a landslip, or part of a glacier goes crashing into the sea because*

of global warming. She did so much for me, especially when it came to looking after the house and cooking. The kitchen was her domain, and she was an excellent cook. I'm afraid I don't even know how to boil an egg! Today my good friends Ash and Di (Ash is the pastor of our church) came to give me my first cookery lesson. We went to the supermarket and bought the ingredients, then we cooked a stir-fry meal and then we ate it together. It was a great lesson for me and such an enjoyable time of fellowship with two very special people.

---

13 August
Had a lovely day with friends down in Derbyshire, and felt I was wrapped in a warm blanket of love. En route, I called in to Boundary Mill, and I discovered I love kitchenalia almost as much as stationery. I bought a special knife for cutting tomatoes, a brush for cleaning pans, an ice cream scoop and a timer to help me remember how long things have been in the oven. How times have changed!

---

18 August
Really enjoyable walk around Pugneys Country Park near Wakefield with my good friend Andy. I have been past many times but never visited until now. After a grey and overcast morning, it was a beautiful afternoon, made all the more special by a good walk, stimulating conversation and an above average coffee. I am realising how healing good friendships are for me during this recovery phase. I am blessed to have so many people who are willing to spend time with me and give me a listening ear right now.

---

19 August
Went for a walk this afternoon in the local park with David, a good friend who has often helped me on my retreats. He took a beautiful photo of me, which is full of meaning. In it I am walking down an avenue of very tall poplar trees and the sunlight is just breaking through the overhead canopy where the branches meet. Much of the

shot is in the shadows, and as it is taken from behind, the path is stretching out ahead of me. No one else is there; it is a moment of solitude and reflection, of walking alone.[3]

As soon as I saw it, some words sprang into my mind, as if a word from God for me at this time:

> Alone, but not alone
> From the shadows into the light
> Keeping to the straight path

I think these words are meant to guide me through my grief journey so I will hold on to them and continue to ponder them.

27 August

Sometimes the words you are reading leap off the page and hit you between the eyes. Suddenly it is as if their meaning explodes within your mind, and you see a truth you have never seen before. It is a moment of deep insight, of knowing something that will change the way you understand yourself and the whole of life.

This happened to me this morning when I read these words:

> There is possibly no more difficult experience than to lose someone you have loved and cared about. There is no greater loss than to be separated from someone who loved you and cared about you.[4]

These two simple sentences affected me profoundly, and I think they will inform the whole course of my grief journey from this point onwards. It's the second sentence that is striking and a loss not so easily recognised or admitted. They reveal to me the heart of the matter as far as my own loss is concerned – I can continue to love Evelyn, but she cannot continue to love me.

The first sentence is not a surprise. This is how I previously understood grief and its impact on those left behind. When Evelyn passed away, I lost the person I loved the most in the world – my closest friend and soulmate, my lover and the mother of my children, my companion on life's journey and the one I trusted most in the world. While that is hard, my love for her will continue, albeit differently. I can no longer tell her I love her or express that love through my actions, but in my heart, I know I will always love her and that I will never forget her. She will live on in my heart. That first sentence continues, albeit in a different way.

It is the second sentence that pierces my heart, for I realise now that the love and care I received from Evelyn is lost forever. That affects me profoundly, for she loved me without condition. With her I felt safe, accepted, valued and appreciated. Her love gave me a sense of worth and security and satisfied a deep longing in my heart to be known and loved completely. Where to find that love again? Yes, I know that God loves me completely and that his love is more certain that any human love could ever be. But God's love is expressed to us so often in the love of another person, and now that love has gone. I feel there is a hole in my heart, and now I know why.

---

28 August

It looks as if I will not be able to go to Australia to see my son Alistair and his family as expected, certainly not before Christmas, so what am I going to do with my time? I think it gives me the opportunity to put into print my reflections from the period when we heard that Evelyn's condition was terminal to the time she passed away. I posted almost every day during those days on Facebook, and my postings were well received. Our story may be able to help others on a similar journey during the pandemic. It may mean self-publishing, which will be an adventure in itself.

There is hope

> Brothers and sisters, we do not want you to be uninformed about those who sleep in death, so that you do not grieve like the rest of mankind, who have no hope.
> 1 THESSALONIANS 4:13

The apostle Paul is not saying here that we should not grieve. Grief, as we have seen, is a natural human response to loss of any kind, especially to bereavement. Although some people may want us to minimise our loss, it is healthier to acknowledge the enormity of what has happened and not be afraid of our emotions.

What he is saying is that because of our hope in Christ, we need not grieve with the empty despair of those who have no confident belief in the afterlife, no assurance of heaven to temper their sadness. As Christians we know that Jesus has conquered death and that dying is the way we pass from this life on earth to life in heaven with him. Thus, the death of a believer is both sad and joyous at the same time. Christ has conquered the grave and removed the sting of death (1 Corinthians 15:54–58).

We can think of dying as 'falling asleep', only to wake up in the presence of Christ. In heaven there will be no more death or mourning or crying or pain, and God will wipe away every tear from our eyes (Revelation 21:3–4). When we know these truths, we can comfort one another with the reassurance they offer. We will still grieve, feel sad and shed our tears, but not forever and not out of a sense of hopeless despair. Healing is possible.

Making adjustments

The loss of our spouse means that we have to adjust to the new reality of life without the one who meant so much to us and played such an important role in our life. That change begins on day one, but as Bill Webster says, 'It is often not until we have finally come to the point of realising that our loved one has gone and will not return that we begin to adjust to a new environment in which that relationship is missing.'[5]

There will be practical adjustments – who will cut the grass, do the washing, clean the car or take care of online banking? We may have to learn new skills simply to get by and will discover that we now have more to do than before.

We will have to adjust emotionally and come to terms with life on our own. There will be a change from 'we' to 'me' and from 'our' to 'my'. Loneliness can be described as the sense of isolation caused by the absence of a much-valued relationship, and we may feel its sting for the first time. The challenge will be to go on and learn to live separately.

Our social life may well be affected. Before we could do things as a couple, but now we may need to go to places alone. This takes courage and the temptation will be to withdraw ourselves from social events, whether church or special occasions.

We will certainly miss the love and affection that we received from our loved one and will have to adjust to being single again – a widow or a widower. Other people may not know how to relate to us, and we will certainly be classified differently in their eyes now we are no longer part of a couple. We will have to find our identity again given our new status in life.

All of this can seem very daunting, but fortunately we don't have to do everything at once. We can move forward step-by-step and one day at a time.

SEPTEMBER 2020

Stabilising

Denial and anger

> Then [Job] fell to the ground in worship and said, 'Naked I came from my mother's womb, and naked I shall depart. The Lord gave and the Lord has taken away; may the name of the Lord be praised.' In all this, Job did not sin by charging God with wrongdoing.
> JOB 1:20–22

Job suffered unimaginable losses, with the destruction of his flocks and the death of his children. Such suffering is beyond our ability to conceive. Most of us will, mercifully, never have to face such multiple tragedies.

At first sight Job seems to meet his tragedies with commendable faith, choosing to worship God rather than blame him for what has happened. And yet, as I read the story, I can't help but think Job's response is made in that period of grief when he is in shock and numbed by what has happened. He too easily falls into worship and acceptance of God's will, and this seems unnatural after such major losses. This is a temptation faced by those of us with a strong basis of faith in our lives – we may be too quick to see God's hand in our loss, responding out of our sense of unreality rather than facing up to the significance of our loss.

I say this because, after a period of silent mourning with his friends, Job bursts out in a tirade of anger against God, cursing the day of his birth (Job 3:1). His pent-up rage is suddenly released, and his friends take the brunt of his outburst. Most of the remainder of the book describes his complaint against God. Although this may be offensive to many believers, it seems a more understandable response to his earlier losses and the personal affliction he also suffers.

Both denial and anger are part of a normal grieving process. Denial can mean that we minimise what has happened and want to move on too quickly. Anger shows that the reality of what has happened to us has at last sunk in and is a necessary part of the healing process. It may be projected on to God, the medical profession, even the deceased person, or anyone who happens to be nearby. At least when we are angry we have started to get in touch with our feelings, which marks the start of the pathway to acceptance and healing.

Secondary losses

The death of a loved one is our main loss, but over time we discover other secondary losses as we begin to realise the many ways in which that person impacted us and contributed to our life. A secondary loss happens as a consequence of the primary loss and is no less important or painful. We find ourselves being impacted in unexpected ways as things we once took for granted no longer happen – for example, changing a light bulb, remembering birthdays, cutting the grass or writing the Christmas cards.

It is worth taking time to stop and consider what we have lost in addition to the presence of our loved one. It may be companionship – the loss of a helper, confidante and lover. It may be the things they did for us and the knowledge they had, the particular skills they possessed and from which we benefitted. We may discover that our shared history has gone, too, except in your own memory, and there is no longer someone with whom we can digest news or discuss points of view. Decision making can be harder because now we have to decide on our own with no one to help us weigh up the alternatives.

Effective grief work is better not done alone, and to get through we will need the help of family and friends, even occasionally a counsellor or specialist helper. Many people find it helpful to belong to a support group where they can meet others in a similar position and learn more about the grief process. Asking for help is not a sign of weakness, but of wisdom.

2 September
Just discovered that when I feel sad it helps to go for a long walk, even in torrential rain and with passing motorists doing their best to splash me in the downpour. Just singing in the rain. Then you arrive home to find a parcel from a good friend with a canvas print of the lovely photo he took of you a few days ago. A reminder to keep praising the Lord no matter how we are feeling.

3 September
On my way to Scarborough to stay with my sister Jean and her husband for a week. Strange feeling to be going away on holiday without Evelyn. It is one of those pleasurable moments that I should be able to enjoy, but a feeling of guilt creeps up on me. 'Why should I be able to do this, and Evelyn can't?' I ask myself. And also a sense of loneliness, of absence, with a joyful experience ahead but no one with whom to share it.

6 September

Yesterday we spent the morning in Whitby, walking along the windswept West Cliff. It was both beautiful and bracing. After a picnic in the car, we set off for Saltburn, a seaside place of special memories, where Jean and I spent many childhood holidays. My mother was born nearby, and my grandfather worked in the local ironstone mines before moving south to the Yorkshire coalfield.

We enjoyed seeing some familiar sights – the coastguard cottages where Mum grew up, the Ship Inn, the beach with its pier, the promenade and the little steam train puffing its way along the hidden valley. We looked for the old iron bridge, but it is no more. The place was heaving with people and not too safe in these virus days, so we walked along the pier, which was quieter and sanitised by a fierce wind.

After that we strolled along the hidden valley beside its babbling brook. Sheltered from the wind, it felt like a different day. At the end of the trail we discovered a little cafe, where we had a delicious coffee and cake before returning to the car. On the way back Jean nearly capsized her mobility scooter as she turned a sloping bend, a bit of unwelcome excitement. Fortunately, her husband David and I caught her just in time.

It was an afternoon for reminiscing and sharing memories. What a gift memory is, and how important sometimes to be able to think about and appreciate the past. But it occurred to me that we had also made some new memories to add to the bank of our personal histories. Maybe in the future we will talk about yesterday with a hint of nostalgia too.

Evelyn and I had also visited Saltburn about two years ago, and of course yesterday I was remembering that happy day as well when I had shared my childhood stories with her. I have a lifetime of memories made together with Evelyn, and recalling special times gives me great joy. But it is also time to make new memories as well, and yesterday now has its place in my memory bank.

10 September
So grateful to my sister Jean and her husband David for a great week in Scarborough. Days out, lots of laughter, good food and company... All very healing and restoring. Now on the way home and back to my own cooking!

13 September
Someone mentioned to me that if I want to learn how to cook, a good starting-point would be Delia Smith's book with that very title, <u>Delia's How To Cook</u>. I was telling my daughter Debbie about this, and she remembered that she had a copy which we had given her many years ago. It is now in my possession. But look how it begins – I thought this was very pertinent and meaningful:

> *If you want to learn how to cook, start with eggs. That's my advice. Eggs, are, after all, a powerful symbol of something new happening – new life, a new beginning. But there is another reason. Somehow eggs have become an equally negative symbol. When someone says, 'Oh, I can't even boil an egg,' what they are actually saying is, 'I can't cook anything at all.'*[6]

18 September
It's a birthday weekend. Today, granddaughter Emily in Perth (Australia) has her first birthday. Then on Sunday my wonderful daughter Debbie has a slightly bigger birthday. This will be the first time without Evelyn. We will have a meal together this evening. Normally Evelyn would provide a chocolate cake and candles. The cake I can provide, but where are the candles? I've no idea where to find them. We will miss her today, for sure!

21 September

Today's devotional from Lectio 365 *has a focus on the life of Henri Nouwen (1932–96).[7] This Roman Catholic priest and spiritual director enabled many people through his writings to discover for themselves the unconditional love of God. At the heart of his message is the reminder that our identity is based on our relationship with God – we are his deeply loved children. Discovering this truth some years ago revolutionised my ministry. I have a feeling that in this period of bereavement, when my identity is once more shaken, I need to enter even more fully into the reality that God delights over me with singing, that I am still the apple of his eye.*

23 September

For my 70th birthday last March, our church friends gave me a gift of money with the suggestion that I buy a picture that I have long admired – Kissing the Face of God *by American artist Morgan Weistling. It shows Mary tenderly holding the infant Jesus and looking at him with the kind of maternal love that gives a child a strong feeling of being safe and secure.*

The canvas arrived from the States just before we went into the care home, so it lay unattended for several months. Eventually I got round to having it framed, and yesterday collected it from the shop. Now it is hanging in a place of honour in the house. It speaks to me of love and devotion (on Mary's part), but also of humility, sacrifice and identification (on the part of Jesus).

This morning I was reading a short email on the theme of transition from the London Institute of Contemporary Christianity, written by Bev Shepherd, which by coincidence is about the obedience of Mary. She writes:

When God initiates change in our lives, it can be tempting to want to know every detail of the plan. How is this to come about? What if I face opposition? Sometimes God, in his mercy, chooses to give us the full project plan; at other times just the first step. What God looks for, though, is our 'Yes' – 'I am the Lord's servant. May your word to me be fulfilled.'[8]

In my own time of transition, I seek to renew my love for God and to embrace his will for the next stage of my life.

26 September

All the time I was with Evelyn in the care home in the period leading up to her death, I shared my thoughts and feelings on Facebook, often with biblical reflections that seemed relevant. These had a good response, and I was encouraged by friends to publish them. Since I have not been able to make the planned trip to Australia to see Alistair and his family, I have decided to collect these into book form and to self-publish the story. Self-publishing seems straightforward enough and not as expensive as I thought. With my nephew Chris to help with the technicalities and my friend Mike to do proofreading, I think we can make a good job of it.

28 September

Just looking ahead this morning to the month of October and the entries carefully written in our calendar by Evelyn of birthdays, anniversaries and significant events. Every year she would painstakingly copy and update this information into a new calendar, and I hope to follow the same practice. Otherwise I will forget some important dates!

It is always touching to see her familiar handwriting, but as I read down I was struck by the entry for 29 October where she had written: 'Dr Scott Chest swelling 2015.' That was the recurrence of breast cancer, and a reminder now that we had five bonus years to enjoy together. Yes, it was hard at times, but we still managed a trip to Australia, had some wonderful holidays here (including two with all the family) and I think used the time we had wisely. But for us all it is a reminder to treasure the time with those we love and make the most of every day that God gives us. Let's not take family and friends for granted. Life is too uncertain to become complacent.

Even in the valley

> Even though I walk through the darkest valley, I will fear no evil, for you are with me; your rod and your staff, they comfort me.
> PSALM 23:4

Psalm 23 presents us with a picture of God as the good shepherd, a reminder of his tender care for his sheep, the people of God. The shepherd in his wisdom leads his sheep towards green pastures, but sometimes the way may pass through dark and frightening valleys. Then it is that the sheep must trust the shepherd.

The words 'darkest valley' are often translated as 'the valley of the shadow of death', and it is easy to see the connection. Bereavement casts a very dark shadow over us, the shadow of loss and sadness. We find ourselves passing through a very narrow passage in life, and we feel afraid and lonely. At such a time it is good to know the comforting presence of God.

When we are grieving it is not always easy to feel or sense the presence of God, especially when we are feeling numb because of our pain. God is there, but we may find it hard to recognise his presence, to register his closeness. Our emotions may well be all over the place and our concentration lacking. We may feel abandoned, deserted even by God.

At such times it is good to remember that God's presence is often communicated to us through other people. Those who come to us in our hour of need with a friendly word, a comforting embrace or an act of kindness are in fact agents of God. Their compassion and concern are expressions of God's compassion and concern. He is there because they are there.

Furthermore, just as the presence of clouds does not negate the existence of the sun, so the fact that our wounded emotions cannot register God's presence does not mean he has ceased to exist or turned his back on us. The day will come when the clouds part and the sun shines again. Or as the prophet promised, 'the sun of righteousness will rise with healing in its rays' (Malachi 4:2).

Possessions

One of the immediate questions we face on losing our spouse is what to do with their belongings. This is a very personal question, and people will vary in their responses. While initially we may choose to leave their things untouched and intact, eventually most people realise they need to do something. Sometimes practical considerations, such as the need for space or to tidy up, may make this a priority. At other times it may be the difficulty of being surrounded by so many reminders of our loved one that motivates us to do something. We may also realise that as long as we cling on to their belongings, we may be delaying our own recovery.

A common suggestion is to tackle this difficult task in stages. Initially, and when we feel ready, we can remove any specialist medical equipment there may have been, plus any clothing and items that are of no value. Often a relative or friend can help with this. Old shoes and coats might be in this category.

Then, a bit later, we can attend to the more personal and valuable items. Some of these we may want to offer to friends and relatives as keepsakes; others we may pass on to charity shops or good causes. Some items we may be able to sell.

Finally, and further on in the process, we may deal with those items with emotional value and sentimental attachment. This is the hardest stage. Some we may choose to keep in a memory box – a few clothes, jewellery, some photos, letters, mementos – whatever is most important to you. This may also be the time to clear out a bedroom, study or shed. We need to be strong at this point, and again the help of a friend can make it a little easier.

OCTOBER 2020

Learning

Is there blessing in loss?

Blessed are those who mourn, for they will be comforted.
MATTHEW 5:4

When the enormity of our loss first hits us, we cannot imagine that there is anything good about the experience. In the early stages of grief, the pain and heartache we experience do not feel like a blessing, so what does Jesus mean when he makes this bold assertion?

Perhaps our attention should be on the word 'comforted'. The blessing of God comes to us in the way we are comforted by family and friends, and even strangers, in our time of need. I am reminded of a story told by a Methodist minister called upon to visit a bereaved lady who was deeply upset by her sudden loss. 'Where is God in this?' she challenged. He thought for a moment before he replied, and then said wisely, 'Perhaps he is here, in the comfort of your friends.' He pointed to another lady, sitting with her arm around her distraught friend. 'There,' he said, 'is the presence of God.'

Most of us receive amazing support like this in the early stage of grief, but such intensity of help is not sustainable. People have jobs to attend to, families to be cared for and a life of their own to live. Eventually we will need to find strength for ourselves, and that strength is found in God, because he has promised to never leave us or forsake us. This assurance, from Hebrews 13:5, reads like this in the Amplified version:

> I will never [under any circumstances] desert you [nor give you up nor leave you without support, nor will I in any degree leave you helpless], nor will I forsake or let you down or relax my hold on you [assuredly not]!

We can have such confidence because of the character of God. It is his nature to comfort, to impart strength and grace to us, to fortify us and uphold us.

How does God do this? By the work of his Spirit within us – the Spirit who is a comforter, the one who draws alongside us in our times of need (John 14:16, 26). It is the Spirit who gives us faith to believe God's promises, who reminds us of God's love, who gives us peace in our innermost being even in the midst of our loss. This is the blessing that Jesus is speaking about. We would never know such comfort, such closeness of his presence, had we not found ourselves in the valley of grief.

Stages of grief (part 1)

Elisabeth Kübler-Ross famously identified five stages in the grieving process, although she did not intend them as stops on some linear timeline of grief, as they are often presented. Grief is as individual as our lives and follows no neat pattern or orderly timescale.

1 *Denial* – our first response to death may be shock and denial, a sense of unreality or numbness. There is the feeling that this cannot possibly be true. It is not so much the denial of the actual death, but more the feeling that it is a bad dream or a temporary state of affairs, as if the person has gone away but will return.

2 *Anger* – once the bubble of unreality has burst, we may feel angry about what has happened. This may be directed towards oneself for not responding better, the person who has died for leaving us, God for allowing it or other people for not properly understanding or supporting us. Anger is one of many emotions that begin to surface once the numbness wears off, including sadness, panic, loneliness and grief. Anger is an expression of pain and of our trying to make sense of what has happened. We did not want this to happen, and someone must be to blame.

3 *Bargaining* – we may find ourselves trying to negotiate a way back to normality, and thinking 'If only…' or 'What if?' We have the feeling that we would give anything to have our loved one back again, that we would like a second chance. We long for things to return to how they used to be. There is a yearning and longing for what we once had.

Remember that the stages were never meant to pack messy emotions into tidy boxes. There is no standard way to grieve, and no one-size-fits-all when it comes to the grieving process.

3 October

Words of wisdom in today's paper from Marcelo Bielsa, the Leeds United manager:

> *The moments in my life when I have improved are closely related to failure. The moments in my life when I have regressed are closely related to success. Being successful deforms us as human*

beings. It relaxes us. It plays tricks on us. It makes us worse
individuals. It feeds our egos. Failure forms us, makes us more
solid, brings us closer to our convictions. It makes us more
coherent.[9]

Of course, no one wants to fail all the time, but this reminds us
that we can learn from our failures and must not be carried away
by success. I think the same is true of suffering, and especially
bereavement and loss in any form. How we respond to these
challenges is crucial. Hardship is far better for the soul than a life
of ease. Adversity is what God most often uses to shape the soul
and release the fragrant life of Christ from within us.

---

7 October

Tonight I attended via Zoom a grief recovery support programme
from an organisation called GriefShare on 'Loss of a spouse'.[10] For
me it is important to learn more about what grief looks like. Yes,
I have grieved before, having lost both my parents and two of my
siblings (plus their partners). But losing your spouse is entirely
different, and I know I need help. The course was really helpful,
giving an overview of what to expect. The key point? That everyone's
grief is unique. It's important not to compare my grief, or my
response to that grief, to that of others. The way we grieve is as
unique as our fingerprints.

---

13 October

It's been three months since Evelyn passed away, and I was warned
that this might be the period when the reality of my loss hit me.
I can see that this is true. I have a sudden awareness that Evelyn
has now 'gone' and will not return.

While the days go quickly, overall it feels to me like a long time since
she died. People say, 'It's still early days,' and I guess that is true,
but it doesn't feel like that. Quite the opposite. Then again, friends

say, 'You've got plenty of time ahead of you,' but it doesn't feel like that to me either. Having seen my spouse pass away, and two of my siblings, and having had a brush with death myself, I don't see my future stretching out endlessly before me. My concept of time has radically changed. I don't see time as I did before, which is strange, and not everyone can understand that.

---

14 October

In this period of transition, I am having to make many adjustments. We have had two cars for years, because Evelyn needed her own transport when I was away with my work. So there have always been two cars on the driveway. Today though there is only one, The Grey One. I said goodbye to The Red One on Saturday, and it was sad. No point having two cars, is there? So today when I stepped outside the back door something seemed wrong, not quite right. I thought for a moment, then realised there was only one car, The Grey One. The Red One will be there no more. It's a visual reminder of how my world is changing, has changed.

---

16 October

Disappointed that my planned trip to Australia to see Alistair and family can't go ahead because of visa restrictions. So many of my plans for this period of recovery have been thwarted, but we keep smiling, knowing God is in control. On to plan B now – a cold, damp winter in England, dark nights and lockdown! But I have lots of thoughts and ideas, so watch this space.

---

17 October

Some good news today. I have been declared non-diabetic, which is a big relief. Diabetes came on during my stay in intensive care with Covid-19 last June, possibly as a result of the stress I was under and the medication I was on. I have been on insulin injections twice daily ever since. No more jabs now, but I will still watch my diet.

This news completes my healing from the virus, a wonderful answer to prayer. I am so fortunate, especially when so many have serious side effects, often referred to as 'long Covid'.

19 October
More good news. My latest book, <u>Mentoring Conversations</u>, has just been released by BRF. It has 30 topics that might usefully form the basis for a conversation in a mentoring context. I had finished the manuscript at the back end of 2019 and all I have had to do since is work on the proofs. It is beautifully produced, and I like the feel of the book – it makes you want to read it.

20 October
I had hoped to spend a few days in Penhurst Retreat Centre, in Sussex, in November, but just read that they are not receiving guests from Tier 2 areas (where I am), so another disappointment. I had also hoped to visit Scotland with my brother-in-law to see some of Evelyn's relatives, but that also now cannot happen. I am reminded of the poem by Laura Sophia Soole which seems timely:

> *Disappointment – His appointment;*
> *Change one letter, then I see.*
> *That the thwarting of my purpose*
> *Is God's better choice for me.*
> Laura Sophia Soole (unknown–1927)

21 October
Tier 3 restrictions began, which means we cannot travel outside of our area and must wear masks in shops (only essential shops are now open). I began the full online GriefShare programme tonight, put on by a church in Cambridge. It is a video-based course, but with a small group discussion. It seemed very well produced, but there was too much content for me to digest and those involved on

screen seemed to talk too quickly for my liking. Not sure if I will continue with it.

24 October

During the current lockdown my friend Dave Bilbrough has been live-streaming a Saturday concert called Homespun. *Dave's songs introduced me to the idea of grace, the knowledge that God's love is unconditional. I have the highest regard for Dave and his wife Pat, so today it was a privilege to be interviewed on his programme. We talked about the new book and my experience of bereavement. I don't mind talking about my grief journey. It is always good to tell our story, and if it encourages others, even more worthwhile.*

26 October

As you know, I have had the joy of seeing many of my books published, like Mentoring Conversations *last week, but I have never been as excited as I am to tell you about an even newer book called* Finding Refuge. *Why am I so excited, and just a little proud?*

Because this is the first book I have self-published (with the help of my nephew Chris and a good friend, Mike). It is not perfect, but it looks great and it reads well. But mostly I am delighted because it is the story of the time that Evelyn and I spent together over the months as she came to the end of her life, so it is deeply personal. I have taken the Facebook posts that I made during this period, which many of you appreciated so much, and formed them into a book which I hope will be a source of inspiration and comfort during this current time of pandemic and lockdown.

Debbie Hawker says in the foreword:

> *This book contains Tony's reflections as he wrote them in a blog at the time. As his friends read them, we cried and we sometimes laughed (especially reading about his virtual church*

experiences). Amidst suffering and sorrow, Tony brings hope and love. The love he has for Evelyn; love from nurses, doctors, carers and chaplains; love shown by friends; and overall, the love of God. In the darkest of times, Tony draws deeply from the Bible and brings out new insights. He demonstrates how the scriptures remain relevant to daily life today.[11]

28 October

Decided to give the GriefShare course a second chance. I do wish we could meet in person, but that is not possible, but at least we get the chance to share in the break-out groups. Tonight, we learned about the challenges of grief and why grief can seem overwhelming at times. Also, we were reminded to take care of ourselves during this time of mourning – <u>d</u>rink to stay hydrated, <u>e</u>at regularly, <u>e</u>xercise and <u>r</u>est (DEER). Sounds like good advice.

31 October

After a busy day yesterday, I thought I would have slept well, but no – wide awake at 1.30 am. Got up, had a cup of tea and read a bit of <u>Mentoring Conversations</u>. Then decided at 2.00 am to have a hot shower, since there was no one in the house to disturb. That's a first for me, showering at 2.00 am. I can add it the list of other firsts we talk about on the bereavement course.

Joy instead of mourning

> The Spirit of the Sovereign Lord is on me… He has sent me to bind up the broken-hearted… to comfort all who mourn, and provide for those who grieve in Zion – to bestow on them a crown of beauty instead of ashes, the oil of joy instead of mourning, and a garment of praise instead of a spirit of despair.
> ISAIAH 61:1–3

There is no doubt that when we lose someone we love dearly, sadness and sorrow can become our constant companions, wrapping themselves around us like a blanket of grief. We can feel overwhelmed with the pain, as if our heart will break. We can lose all hope for the future and despair of ever feeling normal again.

Here is a reminder that God is aware of us and our need and will come to help us in our suffering. Here is a promise of healing and restoration, an assurance that we will find a way through and we will recover our equilibrium.

The Bible states clearly that the Lord is our healer, and that means emotionally as well as physically (Exodus 15:26). It is right to ask God to heal us of our pain and sorrow. If we are unable to pray ourselves, we can ask others to pray for us and to ask God to fulfil his promises given here to bestow his healing upon us. Not that this is a magical formula by which we can speed up the grieving process. No, it does not mean that. What it does mean is that we are enabled to grieve well and, with the passing of time and the impartation of God's grace, to find our joy returning and our spirit lifted. Once again there will be a sparkle in our eyes, a smile on our face and a song of praise on our lips.

Stages of grief (part 2)

The work of Elisabeth Kübler-Ross on grieving has been developed more recently by grief expert David Kessler.[12] He is at pains in the book *On Grief and Grieving* to stress that the stages of grief are not meant to describe an automated, mechanical process. Life and grief are too unpredictable for that. At the same time, we can recognise certain patterns in the grief process even if the overall experience is very untidy.

4 *Depression* – eventually the stark realisation sinks in that our loved one will not return and that they have gone for good from our lives. This can throw us into depression, which is a normal and natural response to death, but not a form of mental illness. Sadness and low mood are unavoidable. We may feel despair and lose hope for the future. The world without our loved one can seem very bleak. Such feelings of depression are not permanent, however, and will eventually pass.

5 *Acceptance* – finally we begin to learn to live with the reality of the new situation. We do not like it, but we accept this is the way it is, and while we cannot change it, we can adapt to it and learn to readjust. Thus begins the process of reintegration, putting the pieces back together again and learning to live with the loss. Gradually, in our own time, we come to peace with what has happened. We do not forget but we are no longer consumed by the loss.

There is no particular timescale to the different stages, and we can move in and out of them in no particular order, but these are the common ingredients of most experiences of grief.

NOVEMBER 2020

Understanding

Near to the broken hearted

> The Lord is close to the broken-hearted and saves those who are crushed in spirit…
> He heals the broken-hearted and binds up their wounds.
> PSALM 34:18; 147.3

The connection between our body and our emotions is well known. The body responds to what we are feeling, especially when we are stressed or greatly upset. After bereavement our immune system is often weakened and we become prone to minor illnesses. We may feel tired and fatigued. In extreme cases it is possible to die of a broken heart. A bereaved person is six times more likely to suffer heart disease than others. Traumatic life events, such as the death of a spouse, can cause 'broken heart syndrome'. The syndrome occurs when a surge of stress hormones causes short-term heart muscle failure. The condition is usually treatable, but it can be fatal. Thankfully it is quite rare.

Mostly when we speak of being broken-hearted, it is a metaphor for the enormity of our loss and the resulting pain and sadness. It feels as if it will never go away and that we will never be back to normal.

However, as human beings we have an amazing capacity to recover from trauma and to find our equilibrium again.

God is especially close to those who feel broken-hearted and crushed by life's events. The knowledge of his love and care can play a significant part in our healing and recovery. Our wounds will heal with time, and even though they may leave a scar, with God's help we can find the strength to start again.

The Australian bush fires of 2019 devastated huge areas of the country, obliterating trees and wildlife. Yet within weeks new shoots of growth were to be seen sprouting from charred tree stumps – nature has an incredible way of regenerating. However great our loss, and whatever the magnitude of our emotional reaction, we too have the capacity to recover and to enjoy life once more. There is hope.

Guilt and regret

Guilt is a troublesome emotion, but it seems to be a familiar companion of those who grieve, for many different reasons. The best way to deal with it is to openly acknowledge it, to name the feeling and identify the reason behind it. Mostly we will discover our guilt is not justified, but if we did do something wrong, we can ask for and receive God's forgiveness. We need also to come to the place of forgiving ourselves and accepting that in being human we have weaknesses and limitations and sometimes we fail.

We may blame ourselves for what has happened and regret that we did not do more to prevent it. We may wish we had valued the person more and spent more time with them. Perhaps we didn't get the chance to say a proper 'goodbye', and maybe our relationship was strained at the end. None of this can be changed, however, and it is fruitless to go on punishing ourselves with condemnation. Guilt can cripple us if we allow it to.

As we begin to recover and start to enjoy life again, we may feel guilty that we are happy, thinking that such emotions are inappropriate and a denial of our love for the deceased. We may ask, 'Why am I here able to enjoy this and my spouse is not?' As time goes on and we perhaps start a new relationship, we may feel that to love another person is a betrayal of the love we had before. It is not; a new relationship in time is a normal and healthy development.

It is important to distinguish between true guilt (we did something wrong) and false guilt (feeling guilty even though we did nothing wrong). Talking in confidence to a counsellor, pastor or wise friends may help us to discern what we are feeling and to respond appropriately.

4 November
I'm really getting into the GriefShare course now and enjoying the small group after the teaching session. We can talk openly there about our thoughts and feelings. There is no map for the grief journey, but we can have some goals – to accept the reality of what has happened, to express our emotions appropriately, to establish a new identity without our partner and to depend on God.

5 November
I've been feeling overly busy recently and wondered why. Then, last night during the GriefShare course came a flash of insight – when you lose your spouse you end up doing the work of two people. And that's right. Cooking, washing, ironing, shopping and gardening have all been added to my to-do list, all things normally taken care of by Evelyn. Now I'm trying to do all these things plus what

I did before. No wonder I feel a bit overloaded. Time for a rethink. Perhaps lockdown will help me regain the balance and see where to scale back.

---

6 November

A mutual friend put me in touch with Ian, an Anglican minister whose wife died a few years ago. It was helpful to talk with him today and to learn from his experience which he has reflected on in a self-published book, <u>What Is Life Without My Love?</u> *There he writes:*

> *Grief can either turn inwards in bleak devastation or outwards in redemptive action. There is always a period of devastation in which the question, 'What is life without my love?' leads the grieving heart into unmitigated sorrow… How long this darkest period lasts depends on the individual; everyone's experience is different. But the flip side of vulnerability is sensitivity; the experience of loss can open the heart to a new awareness of the pain of others.*[13]

---

8 November

This morning I have the unusual opportunity to hear myself preach! I have pre-recorded a talk for this morning's service at my home church, Ackworth Community Church. This will be the first time I have done any public speaking since the start of the year, so I was a bit nervous, and videoing myself was a new experience too. The last time I was scheduled to preach (in February last year) I had to withdraw because my mind could not focus given all that was happening with the news that Evelyn's condition was terminal. It is good now to be able to concentrate again and discern what God is saying.

The theme this morning is 'Disappointment' – based on Habakkuk 3. All of us have known huge disappointments this year with the effects of the pandemic, but how do we cope? Must we be overwhelmed by our sadness and loss? The prophet says not. We can choose to rejoice even though things are not going well: 'Yet I will rejoice in the Lord, I will be joyful in God my Saviour' (v. 18).

10 November
Disappointment is a form of loss, and with loss there is grief. When our hopes are dashed and things don't work out as we expected, we also experience a grief reaction. In this sense grief is the emotion we feel when we lose something or someone that is important to us. I had been hoping to be on retreat today, but the pandemic restrictions meant I could not travel. Perhaps that's why I feel a little sad today. I was really looking forward to having time to spend with God in company with others.

11 November
It's hard to believe that tonight was the fourth GriefShare session. One of the ladies was very upset tonight. It is perhaps a bit soon for her to be talking about her loss publicly. We started by recognising that the grief journey often seems too long, too hard and too painful. I second that. There was practical advice too about dealing with a loved one's belongings, and the thought that, hard as it is to sort through personal possessions, it actually aids the grief process by putting us in touch with our memories and, therefore, our feelings. The general advice seems to be to do it yourself if possible and at your own pace. I know I still have a lot of things that belonged to Evelyn to sort through.

14 November
One thing we can do during lockdown is to meet up with one person to exercise outside. I am in a rhythm now of walking regularly on Saturday mornings with Cliff, a busy vicar who also appreciates time to chat as we walk, whether that be about faith, football, the

state of the nation or the latest family news! It is all very life-giving to me, and I appreciate his friendship so much.

17 November

Today should have been the start of the annual Mentoring Forum, which I have been organising for several years, but it too has been cancelled. So, there is another loss, a stressful one too. I was not sure until the last minute if I would lose my rather considerable deposit, but I can transfer it forward to next year. Phew! The times of fellowship we have enjoyed at the forum have always been rewarding, and I will miss seeing a very special group of people.

18 November

What surprised me about this evening's GriefShare session was the insight that some of our relationships may change after the death of a loved one. Some friends, for example, may not know how to respond to us because a few don't know what to say or how to relate to us after our loss. Others may be unsure now we are single. They may withdraw and the closeness of the friendship may change. Some people will make insensitive remarks, and we were warned not to take offence. Quite a bit to chew over there. I wonder how my relationships are changing.

19 November

There are friends, good friends and great friends, all of them special in their own way and essential to our well-being. Just been for an invigorating walk with my great friend Jonathan. We have enjoyed more than 20 years of sharing and caring, talking and praying, laughing and joking, hoping and dreaming, encouraging and supporting. If you have such friends, thank God for them and be sure to let them know they are important to you.

20 November

I've been busy this month sending out copies of <u>Finding Refuge</u>, and I am pleased with the response. I have also been selling online my stock of books which I normally take to the events at which I am speaking. It seems better than them sitting in a cold garage over the winter. I'm sure Amazon are not in a panic about my sales, but it is a helpful source of income and has given me a sense of purpose. One interesting story is that a lady ordered a copy of <u>Mentoring Conversations</u> to be sent to the house where she was staying temporarily, but when it dropped through the letter box it was devoured by the owner's dog! I'm sure the dog found it spiritually nourishing!

24 November

Out walking with a friend today when we were stopped by a professional photographer doing a study on how people were exercising during the pandemic. He obviously thought we looked the part because he snapped us braving the elements on a gloomy, damp November day

25 November

I'm enjoying doing the GriefShare course on these cold, dark nights. I can do it from the comfort of my office, and it is stimulating and helpful. The emphasis changed this week from topics that brought us comfort to those that bring hope to help us in moving forward and to answering some of our questions. Tonight was largely about 'Why?' and the questions we may have about our loved one's death. We were encouraged to be honest with God, like Job was, but to continue to trust God – in his sovereignty, his goodness, his presence and his understanding of us.

26 November
Today is my grandson George's ninth birthday. I say 'my' when normally I would say 'our'. It's a very subtle change in language, but a significant one and a recognition that for the first time in his life his grandma will not be lighting the candles on his birthday cake.

Steadfast love

> Because of the Lord's great love we are not consumed, for his compassions never fail. They are new every morning; great is your faithfulness. I say to myself, 'The Lord is my portion; therefore I will wait for him.'
> LAMENTATIONS 3:22–24

Lamentations is generally a sad book, as the title suggests, containing the prophet Jeremiah's outpouring of sadness over the downfall of Jerusalem. Yet at the heart of this lament are these words of reassurance and hope that have brought comfort to many, especially in their grief.

When we are in the midst of grief it is easy to feel overwhelmed, as if sadness will consume us, but when we remember the love of God we find hope to keep going. It may feel as if we will never stop crying or never feel happy again, which is why we need to remind ourselves that God has not stopped loving us. We may have lost the one we loved most in the world, but we are still loved. The nature of God's love is that it is steadfast, it never changes and it doesn't end. And right now, in our grief, we are the focus of that loving attention.

Two words stand out here – 'compassion' and 'faithfulness'. God is full of compassion towards us, feeling for us in our pain. His heart goes out to us, and he truly understands how we feel. He is merciful and will continue to demonstrate his love towards us. Furthermore, he is faithful, utterly committed to us, and nothing will ever change his attitude towards us. This is why each new day will bring tangible reminders of his goodness and grace. We only need eyes to see and the determination to look for them.

Times and seasons

In the process of grieving, it is often said that the first year is the hardest because there are so many 'firsts' – the first time we do something significant without our loved one, visit a favourite place without them or celebrate a special time of the year. These will inevitably bring back many memories that may well make us both happy and sad.

- *Birthdays* – this may focus on the birthday of the one who has died and may for a while intensify the reality that they are no longer with us. But it may also include celebrating our own birthday without them, or the birthdays of our children and grandchildren.

- *Festivals* – times like Easter and Christmas may be full of meaning for us, packed with our own little rituals and memories built up over the years. These treasured moments increase our awareness of the absence of the one we love. A vital piece of the jigsaw is missing. It may be hard to enjoy these occasions as a result. An empty place at the table may be a poignant reminder.

- *Anniversaries* – for those who have been married, wedding anniversaries evoke strong emotions of vows made, promises kept and love enjoyed.

- *Special occasions* – Valentine's Day, public holidays or significant personal milestones can also trigger thoughts and feelings in us that may take us by surprise. We may find our loneliness is accentuated at such times and our sense of loss magnified.

If we prepare ourselves for these red-letter days and anticipate them, it will take some of the sting out of them. Likewise, if we sense it will be difficult for us, we can make plans to be with friends or family who understand our need and can accept it may be difficult for us. Alternatively, if we feel it is better to be alone, that too is fine.

DECEMBER 2020

Accepting

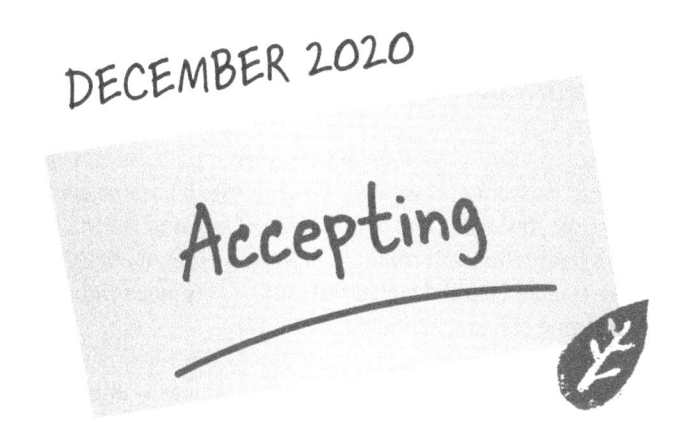

A man of sorrows

He is despised and rejected of men; a man of sorrows, and acquainted with grief: and we hid as it were our faces from him; he was despised, and we esteemed him not.
ISAIAH 53:3 (KJV)

The prophet Isaiah spoke about the Saviour who was to come hundreds of years before it actually happened, describing one who is referred to as the suffering servant. When Jesus began his ministry he stepped into these shoes, fulfilling every word that was written about the coming Messiah. One thing we know about Jesus is that he had experienced suffering and was intimately acquainted with the feelings of grief. This means he can empathise with us in our sorrows.

People often say they understand our pain and know what we are feeling, but in reality they can't always grasp our particular loss – for example, what it is like to lose a spouse. There is a difference between sympathy and empathy. Sympathy means to feel sad for someone who is suffering but in a general way; empathy means to feel again something you yourself have felt before, because you have been in a similar position. Even then everyone's pain is unique and never totally identical, but having experienced something similar gives us a deeper connection that makes our response authentic.

Having lived our life on earth, Jesus has felt our pain. He can empathise with us. He wept at the graveside of his friend Lazarus, because of his own loss, but also sensing the pain of Mary and Martha (John 11:35). It is this identification with us in suffering that qualifies him to be our merciful and faithful high priest, and to pray for us with feeling from the throne of heaven (Hebrews 4:14–16).

We can be sure today that there is one person who truly understands us, who 'gets' what we are going through. And that person is Jesus.

Trapped in grief

Grief is a natural and normal response to the loss of a loved one, and it is not to be hurried or short-circuited. It takes whatever time it requires. Yet there remains a danger that we can get trapped in our grief, so fearful of forgetting our loved one that we refuse to let go. Instead, we surround ourselves with our sadness and refuse to be comforted. There is a time for grief, but we must also be willing to live again.

What keeps us locked in our grief? Most times it happens because we do not want to face the pain. Instead, we choose behaviours that help us avoid the pain. We might hide from it through busyness, losing ourselves in our work. We may try to anaesthetise the hurt through drink, drugs, comfort eating or compulsive buying. But grief work involves facing up to the pain and really feeling our loss. Only when we have accepted the reality can we begin to move forward. We need the courage to walk into the pain if we are to recover.

Often people get stuck because they mistakenly think that healing is the same as forgetting, but the two are not the same. Healing means that we are able to adapt to a new normal without the person, but that doesn't imply that they were not important to us or that we did not love them. Emotions play a big part in getting trapped as well – we will be tempted to feel sorry for ourselves, to wallow in self-pity.

How can we start moving again if we have become becalmed? It will be helpful to talk about our situation with a pastor, counsellor or wise friend. Perhaps there is something specific we can do, like finally dealing with our loved one's belongings if this has become a sticking point. Changing perspective can be liberating too – thinking of what and who we still have, not just what we have lost. We can remember that although our loss is great, life is not over for us yet and God still has a future for us. And of course, we can ask God for his help and the strength we need to take the next step and to choose life.

1 December

So glad that November is behind us. It is my least favourite month, and this year has been particularly difficult. Not only has it been exceptionally cold, dark and damp on many days, but the isolation of lockdown has intensified my sense of loneliness, especially the last week. I'm off to the shops tomorrow! They are open again for a few days before Christmas.

2 December

I'm really appreciating the GriefShare course now, and I always look forward to sharing with the small group after the presentation. This evening was a very moving session, looking at those troublesome emotions – regret, guilt and anger – that seem so common during bereavement. Of those, I think guilt is the one which has troubled me the most, the kind of feeling that is described as 'survivor's guilt' – like 'Why should I be able to enjoy these things when Evelyn can't?' and 'Is it okay to feel happy, have fun and be excited about the future?' Guilt is not a rational feeling, and it can be a bit disturbing.

---

3 December
I wouldn't say I have been lonely during lockdown, but I am starting to enjoy nuisance calls, even the ones where you can't understand a word that is spoken. At least it's contact and a human voice, mostly.

---

4 December
Today's post is not a whinge or a whine, nor a plea for sympathy, so please no virtual hugs or bunches of cyberspace flowers! But it is an insight into the reality of living alone during a time of lockdown and Tier 3 restrictions, for myself and thousands of others.

It is not easy. In fact, it is tough. I consider myself to be fairly resilient and able to manage myself quite well, but yesterday I felt I was beginning to fray around the edges, just a little.

The issue for me revolves around eating alone. Here in Barnsley, we went into Tier 3 about 21 October. This brought with it many restrictions about where we could go and who we could be with. This was followed by actual lockdown, and now a return to Tier 3 again. Social contact has been at a bare minimum for about six weeks now without let-up.

I calculate that, since I eat three meals a day, that is 126 meals in total during this period. I have my 'bubble' of course, with Debbie and her family, for which I am deeply grateful. I eat with them, say, two meals a week, which means I have probably eaten 114 meals alone. No wonder, then, if the seams are coming apart!

But what is the problem with eating alone? Some of you, I know, cooped up at home with little children, would give anything to eat a meal by yourself with no noise or interruption. I understand that;

I have been there. But can you imagine more than a hundred meals, almost consecutively, with no one else there and no conversation?

You see, eating and talking go together. It is one of our basic forms of social interaction. Even if it only involves insights like 'This soup is cold' or 'This toast and jam is delicious', it creates connection with another person, so vital to our well-being. But of course, it can be so much more than that – talking over the day, sharing a problem, reminiscing, planning for the future, and expressing love and affection. It creates a feeling of intimacy or being deeply connected, of belonging. In conversation with another, our existence and worth are validated. We are recognised and acknowledged. So, when you eat alone you are missing all of that, and to my mind that is on par with not being able to have a hug. It is another form of deprivation.

---

7 December

I have had my walking boots for a few years now, and they have been faithful companions. We have walked many miles together during that time, on my daily walks as well as on holiday. They are partly responsible for my physical recovery after Covid-19, so they have a place in my heart. They fit me very well, and we have adjusted to one another. But they are very thin now on the soles and heels, and it is reluctantly time for a change.

On Saturday I bought a new pair. They are clean and smart and fully waterproof. The soles are strong and new. There are no signs of wear and tear. But I know that change is never easy. They will take some time to wear in. They may rub and I may get a blister or two. Occasionally I will long for my old boots and wonder, 'Did I make a mistake?' Hopefully, they will become as much a part of me as my old ones as we tread the miles together. But there is always a risk with something new, isn't there?

Change is never easy in whatever form it comes. But change is inevitable because life does not stand still, and we have to keep adjusting and adapting and being open to fresh winds of the Holy Spirit. Never more so than in these present, troublesome days.

Strangely enough, as I have been meditating on this, my reading today (Isaiah 9) contained a reference to 'Every warrior's boot used in battle... will be destined for burning' (v. 5). Oh dear. I'm sure, like me, warriors were fond of their boots and would be sad to see them go.

---

9 December
It's been GriefShare again tonight, lesson 8. I thought I might find it all too much, but I have enjoyed it. Is that the right word? I like the weekly discipline of being made to think about my grieving and to reflect on my experience. It is all too easy to lose oneself in busyness and not really think about it. On the course we are helped to accept what has happened and to work through our grief. For some the loss of a loved one happened in traumatic circumstances. This means that grieving is far more complicated. There may be flashbacks and nightmares, and it takes a long time to recover.

---

13 December
This week I did something very unusual, a bit out of character.

I have been thinking about buying a new car for some time now, and my search has been focused on the Suzuki Vitara. I have researched it on the internet and even asked people I have met who drive a Vitara about their experience, and it all pointed in the right direction. When I saw one for sale in a garage with the right mileage, colour and specifications, I asked for a test drive, which went well. A good, safe choice.

But on the forecourt of the garage, I saw another car, completely different, and I fell in love with it immediately. I loved the style of

*it, the interior, everything about it. That has never happened to
me before! I asked if I could have a test drive, and it was beautiful.
What's more, the car has low mileage (1,000 miles only, so it is like
new), is still under warranty and has a spare wheel (not many have
these days, but it's important to me). Plus, it was cheaper than the
Vitara. So I bought it! And I pick it up on Monday.*

*Those who know me well may be surprised at this uncharacteristic
spontaneity and wonder why I didn't choose the safer option.
Only time will tell if I made the right decision, but it's good to
be spontaneous sometimes, and in this season of change for me
perhaps I can take a few more risks! God is always at work in us,
loosening us up and opening us to new ways of being. And, as I
mentioned previously, I don't find change easy, but we must embrace
it and be less risk averse.*

*By the way, my new boots are just fine. And for those who want to
know, the car is a Citroën C4 Cactus.*

16 December
*One word summed up tonight's lesson in GriefShare – stuck! It
seems that it is possible to get trapped in our grief, and for our
grief to still feel raw and intense like it was at the beginning, even
several years later. One of the reasons for this is that we can't let go
of our loved one. We fear that we may forget them, but healing does
not mean forgetting. We will always have our memories and we will
still love the person, but we must remember there is a life still to be
lived.*

We have a break from the course now. It will resume in January.

19 December
*Enjoyed a good morning today at Lakeside near Doncaster, on a
bright sunny morning. First a little Christmas shopping, then a walk*

around the lake. It has become one of my go-to places this year. Today I was walking alone rather than with a friend, and I noticed it seemed further and to take longer. When you are walking and talking, you hardly notice the distance or the time.

I am not usually able to think much when I am walking, but today a saying popped into my head: 'If you want to go fast, go alone. If you want to go far, go together.' It made me thankful for all the friends who have encouraged me on my journey this year and helped me to keep going. We can walk alone, and sometimes that's good. But it is easier to be able to walk through life with others. Who has walked with you this year? Do they know that you appreciate their companionship on the journey?

---

24 December

Good morning everyone on this Christmas Eve morning. I am thanking God for all those who connect with me on Facebook – some frequently, some occasionally, some silently and unobserved. Thank you for letting me share my thoughts with you, especially through the trials of 2020. And thank you for your many kind, wise and loving responses. For all the faults of Facebook, this connection has been a major source of encouragement and strength to me.

Evelyn and I had a tradition of opening a few presents on Christmas Eve. It won't be quite the same by myself.

---

25 December

Spent most of the day with Debbie and her family. What excitement for George and Jacob as they opened their presents, and what a feast we had at lunchtime. It was strange without Ev being there, one of those moments that seems incomplete, when you are enjoying life but with a tinge of guilt, sadness and maybe regret. But since the message of Christmas is true, we have this comfort – that in Jesus God took human flesh, became one of us so that he could save us and share in our suffering. The name given to him was Emmanuel, and it means God is with us, whatever our circumstances.

26 December
Just when I thought today may be a difficult day, I am blessed and surprised by someone bringing me a second Christmas lunch and another person promising me a Chinese meal this evening. This is good for my morale, but not for my waistline, which was already affected adversely by yesterday's Christmas lunch at Debbie's. But these days of lockdown during a holiday period are not easy for those living alone.

28 December
Hoping to get back into the groove again today and start on some writing assignments that are waiting for me. I am pleased to have got through the last few days relatively unscathed – the days have been long and a bit lonely because of the Tier 3 restrictions, but also not without some wonderful tokens of God's love and favour. And I have a great sense of good things to come in the year ahead, even if it begins with the constraints of coronavirus still upon us.

31 December
Went out to a local beauty spot to watch the last sunset of 2020. There was nothing remarkable as this most infamous of years came to a welcomed closure, just a normal winter dusk. Strangely I feel no animosity to the year now departing, the year that brought us such words as 'coronavirus' and 'Covid-19', 'pandemic' and 'social distancing', 'lockdown' and 'furlough'. It has been tough for us all, and yet in the darkness a light shines – the presence and grace of God.

Other words have been prominent in my own vocabulary this year, words such as 'kindness' and 'compassion', 'family' and 'friends', 'love' and 'generosity', 'medical skill' and 'prayer', 'healing' and 'recovery'. It has been a year like no other, but it has still had its share of blessing, and we still have so much for which to be thankful. And now there is the prospect of a new year ahead of us and the chance to see what God will do in us and through us in 2021.

God in all things

> And we know that in all things God works for the good of those who love him, who have been called according to his purpose… I am convinced that neither death nor life, neither angels nor demons, neither the present nor the future, nor any powers… will be able to separate us from the love of God that is in Christ Jesus our Lord.
> ROMANS 8:28, 38–39

One amazingly strong foundation for our walk with God is the knowledge of his providence – that is, his ability to weave everything that happens to us into his overall good purpose for our lives. This includes even the bereavement we have experienced, with its pain and loss. One day we will see how God has brought something good out of what at the time may seem to have been painful and difficult to understand.

Death does not have the last word. It is a powerful enemy, and its icy grip touches every life at some time, often many times, but it has been defeated. Christ defeated death by his resurrection and its sting has been removed. Elsewhere Paul quotes the prophet Hosea and declares triumphantly, 'Where, O death, is your victory? Where, O death, is your sting?' (1 Corinthians 15:55, quoting Hosea 13:14). This means that for the believer who dies, death becomes the doorway into heaven and the presence of God. And for those who remain to grieve their loss, there is the comfort of the love of God and the assurance that good will come out of the sadness.

That good is often seen in the change that takes place within us as we experience bereavement. It has a softening effect upon us, making us more humble, more compassionate and more empathetic towards others. But it also inspires some people into action, to start campaigns, to correct injustices, to make sure others do not have to suffer in the way they have. One day we too will look at what has happened in an altogether different way. We will see that God made something good come out of our loss.

Grief as integration

Grief counsellor Lois Tonkin introduced the idea of growing around grief as another way of understanding the grief journey.[14] In this model, grief does not go away, but we integrate it into our life in a way that helps us to continue to live effectively and happily without forgetting our loved one.

It is common for people to think that with time our grief will get smaller until eventually we forget about it altogether and simply get on with life again. In this view, grief is something that we 'get over', as if it were an obstacle in our path to be overcome. Many people find, however, that grief does not go away so easily, and neither do they want it to. The idea of forgetting about their loved one and living as if they never existed is anathema to them, and rightly so.

Rather, we can think of grief as something which is incorporated into our life. It never goes away, but we grow around our grief. The idea is often explained like this. Imagine a circle that represents our life and what we are experiencing. Then we shade in part of the circle to represent our grief – it may well cover the whole circle. Over time the shaded part (our grief) does not get smaller, but the unshaded part (representing us and our life) begins to grow bigger.

This is sometimes called the 'fried egg' model, because that is what it looks like – the white of the egg represents our life and the yolk is our grief. We still grieve, we still miss the person, but we can continue with our life. Our loss becomes part of us; it has been integrated into our very being but not in a way that hinders us or restricts our future growth. We carry forward our love for the person in our memories with thankfulness and gratitude. They continue to be a part of us without preventing us from forming and enjoying new relationships.

What this model also illustrates is that we can grow through our grief and become better people as a result of experiencing loss. We can grow in resilience, courage and bravery and become wiser, more compassionate and increasingly empathetic.

JANUARY 2021

Descending

When we don't understand

> So the sisters sent word to Jesus, 'Lord, the one whom you love is ill.' When he heard this, Jesus said, 'This illness will not end in death. No, it is for God's glory so that God's Son may be glorified through it.' Now Jesus loved Martha and her sister and Lazarus. So when he heard that Lazarus was ill, he stayed where he was two more days, and then he said to his disciples, 'Let us go back to Judea.'
> JOHN 11:3–7

I confess that I do not always understand what God is doing in my life. One thing I have come to realise over the years is that my small, finite mind cannot possibly plumb the depths of the purposes of God. I am often left confused and bewildered at the events in my life, asking, 'Why, Lord?' I have slowly come to accept that I will not always understand God's ways and that I have to be content with not knowing. I am learning to live with a degree of mystery.

Martha and Mary were left bewildered by the delay in the response of Jesus to news of the death of Lazarus. They felt that if he had returned sooner, Lazarus need not have died. Their faith in his love and care for them was severely tested by what happened, and they told him so (John 11:21, 32). Jesus, however, knew what he was doing. The four-day delay confirmed to the Jews that Lazarus was really dead. And all the time Jesus knew that Lazarus would be raised from the dead and that the miracle would be a public declaration that he was indeed the resurrection and the life (v. 25), a pointer to his own resurrection still to come. In the end things worked out well, but the delay and the waiting were painful for the sisters.

Jesus was not indifferent to their heartache. When Jesus saw Mary weeping, he was 'deeply moved in spirit and troubled' (v. 33). Perhaps his weeping at the tomb (v. 35) was an expression not just of his love for his friend Lazarus, but also of his compassion towards the sisters and the ordeal they had been through, as necessary as it was.

This is a great reminder to us that God does not cause us unnecessary pain. Delays and periods of waiting, times of confusion and bewilderment, can all serve to strengthen our faith and develop our trust, if we allow them too. The question is always, 'Can I trust God to do what is good and right?'

Men and women in grief

Do men and women grieve in the same way? It seems not, according to grief counsellor Julia Samuel.[15]

One significant difference is that women more naturally reach out to others for help and support, whereas men are more likely to be reluctant to seek assistance in their grieving. Women tend to be open and expressive and have a greater network of friends offering them emotional support and social connection. Men, in the western world at least, tend to lack this kind of support because of their failure to reach out to their friends, preferring to be 'manly' and deal with it alone. Research shows that in not acknowledging their hurt, anger and confusion, men are more likely to experience higher rates of both mental and physical illness and become more depressed later in their bereavement.

Another significant difference, according to Julia Samuel, is that men are more likely to start a new relationship within a year of their spouse's death, confirming the expression that 'men replace and women grieve'. Women seem more equipped for life alone, whereas men feel keenly and immediately the need for a companion. This can be surprising and shocking to relatives and friends, especially children. There is a danger, too, of hasty responses which may be regretted later.

For both men and women, the loss of a spouse – and therefore a lover – raises the question of the need for sex, which may feel very inappropriate to the newly bereaved and yet may be a surprisingly strong desire. Romance and sex both make us feel alive and valued, which is a great need when you have lost your partner and are aware of your own mortality. Sex (or romantic attachment) is a way of feeling alive again, of feeling loved. It may provide a source of comfort when you feel alone and long to be held and feel safe again. Such a desire need not be selfish. It may in fact be part of the need to give love to another, especially in one who has cared for their spouse during a long illness.

What we need to realise is that following a bereavement, both men and women are emotionally very vulnerable and need to be aware of that lest they behave rashly or unwisely.

---

1 January
Happy New Year everyone. Not just a new day, but a new year ahead – such a gift. And the gift of being alive to enjoy it. Make

this year count for God's glory. Love and appreciate the people around you. Let them know you care. Be kind to all you meet. Live with a generous and grateful heart. Enjoy the moment. Treasure every glimpse of wonder. Be kind to yourself.

6 January

On this Epiphany Day, I was challenged by this beautiful yielding prayer from Carla Harding in Lectio 365*:*

> *King Jesus, You have given me everything. All I can give You is myself. Forgive my sin and refine me like pure gold. Teach me to talk with You and let my prayers be like frankincense, rising to Your throne. And anoint me with myrrh. Help me to walk in Your way of self-emptying, laying-down-my-life love today.*[16]

It was back to the GriefShare course tonight, but this will probably be my last one as we need to restart our midweek home group, which is also on Wednesday. It contained a good reminder that when you lose a spouse, you lose more than just a person. You lose a confidante, lover and friend who played a specific role in your life. We were encouraged to make a list of our 'secondary' losses, those things we have lost as a result of the primary loss of a loved one. There could be as many as 30!

7 January

The spiritual life is a slow journey into the understanding that I am loved unconditionally by God – known for who I am, with nothing hidden or unseen, and yet loved just the same. This is important to remember during bereavement.

8 January

Reminded today that on this day in 1956 a young American missionary called Jim Elliot was martyred as he and his friends sought to reach the Auca Indians in Ecuador with the good news of Jesus. He was only 29 years old and married. His journals reveal a man on fire for God and passionate about discipleship. Through his words, and the writings of his wife Elisabeth, he inspired many others to give their lives in the cause of world mission.

Elisabeth is a good example of someone who faced the loss of a spouse in tragic circumstances and yet found strength in God to carry on, returning to live among the Auca Indians (now called the Huaorani) and inspiring many others to serve as missionaries through her books <u>Through Gates of Splendour</u> and <u>Shadow of the Almighty</u>. Later she hosted a weekly radio programme, which she always began with these words: 'You are loved with an everlasting love, that's what the Bible says, and underneath are the everlasting arms. This is your friend, Elisabeth Elliot…'

11 January
Some days all we can do is to simply put one foot in front of the other and keep moving forward, however slowly.

12 January
Last night at our church prayer meeting, we thought about how church will be different after the pandemic. As we listened to God afterwards, I felt him say, 'It's not that church will be different, it's that you will be different.'

Church will change because hopefully we have changed during this pandemic. Each of us will have been impacted by the pandemic in different ways. But make no mistake about it, the pandemic and the experience of lockdown have changed us, hopefully for the better. And those changes will shape the way we think about church and practise ministry once we are free to meet again.

This is certainly true for me. I am not the same person going into

2021 as I was at the start of 2020. Life has shaped me and deepened me, and I pray this will show in my ministry. I have been sensitised to grief and loss like never before. I have had a brush with death that causes me to value life and not take it for granted. I hope I am a kinder person with a greater empathy for others. I hope I have a better grasp of what is really important and what is secondary. I am more open to change than I have ever been, more willing to accept differences in others and see them as a blessing. I hope all of this will show in my teaching and my writing.

Not many people get the opportunity that I have, to start life again, and I am praying that I will make good choices that will make my later years abundantly fruitful. I don't simply wish to go back to how things were before – I want to live another adventure with God.

It is worth stopping to think about how God is at work in us because we don't want to miss the gift of transformation God is giving us through these difficult days. Let's not waste our sorrows, griefs, losses, sacrifices, hardships and so on. What has God been forming within us? And how will that shape our service for him in the coming days? How will it be different because we are different? What will be new for us as we move forward?

---

13 January

I managed to squeeze in one more session of the GriefShare course, which means I have missed only one. And to think I was unsure about doing it at first! Grief has much to teach us, especially when it comes to valuing relationship, facing trials and how to depend on God. And it can expose things in us too, like our impatience and the way we demand that God does things our way, and according to our time scale.

---

15 January

This morning's devotional from <u>Lectio 365</u> brings me right back to *the basics of how to live the Christian life. Why do we ever wander away from the unforced rhythms of grace?*

Apparently, the Native American Hopi language has a word to describe a life out of balance. They call it 'ko-yaa-nis-qatsi'. It also means 'crazy life', 'life in turmoil', 'life disintegrating' or 'a state of life that calls for another way of living'. In the midst of a life in turmoil, Jesus offers his disciples another way of living – the unhurried, gentle way of meekness that will inherit the earth.

---

18 January

Some time ago I was helping my grandson George into his car seat in the back of my car, when I accidentally banged his head. He started to cry.

'Come on, George, be brave,' I said.

'But I don't want to be brave,' he replied.

I guess we all know that feeling. Sometimes life is hard, and we know we have a need for courage, but somehow, we just don't want to be brave. We would rather give in, surrender to the difficulties and sink in self-pity.

The Bible seems to constantly exhort us to be brave, to be strong, to take heart, to be courageous. And life during and in the wake of a pandemic certainly calls for us to make a courageous response. But occasionally we may feel overwhelmed and ready to give in or give up.

Perhaps you are reading this at just such a moment. Maybe this comes as a message to you from God so that you do not lose heart. He knows you, and he sees your situation. And he speaks to encourage you, as he did to the church at Philadelphia: 'I know that you have little strength' (Revelation 3:8).

He is the compassionate and understanding God who draws alongside us, to give strength to the weary and power to the weak (Isaiah 40:29). You don't have to do anything, simply turn to him in your need and ask for help. You will discover, as the apostle Paul did, that when you are weak, then you are strong. His power will be demonstrated through your weakness. You can do whatever is required of you because he will give you strength.

---

20 January
Crash, bang! Did you hear that noise? It was the sound of my hopes being dashed. Over the last couple of months, I have been building a friendship with a lady and it seemed to be developing well. We have lots of things in common, can talk easily and share a similar spirituality. Although there are some significant differences, we both thought these were not insurmountable, but now it seems they might be. It has hit me very hard and will take some time for me to get over, of that I am sure. I thought I had approached this with an openness to God's leading, and it seemed to be right, but now I'm confused. Did I hear God correctly or not? Perhaps I was trying too hard in my need to find again the deep connection I had with Evelyn. Isn't there a saying, 'The lonely person stretches out their hand too quickly'?

I encouraged George to be brave. Now it's my turn.

---

21 January
Soul refreshing words in this morning's <u>Lectio 365</u> devotional from Aaron White, who works among broken people in Vancouver, Canada:

> God does not just tolerate us. We all come to God in our mess, in need of mercy, and he does not hold his nose and refrain from destroying us. Mercy is not our defence against God's anger; it is Jesus actively pouring out his life and hope for us... God

does not hate us, and he does not leave us to flounder in our trouble.[17]

Lord, hear my cry for mercy.

In tough times I find it helpful to climb to a high point and survey the scene from such a vantage point. Today I did just that when I felt I had let things get out of perspective. A bright and breezy day helped to blow away the cobwebs. Perhaps it's not as bad as it feels?

---

22 January

Today I am lonely. There I said it, and admitted I am incomplete by myself. I am weak, not as strong as I thought. Of course, I can talk to myself, to the plants, to the chair. I can sing to the radio or argue with the TV. I can Skype, Zoom, FaceTime and WhatsApp all day long if I want. But who is there to hold my hand when I am afraid? Who is there to give me a hug when I feel unworthy? Who will kiss me with passion and longing and remind me I'm attractive and desirable?

Who am I? One of thousands of people, men and women, young and old, trapped in the lonely confines of lockdown in the dead of winter. It is taking its toll on even the strongest, sapping the strength of the most resilient.

Lord, in your mercy, reach down and touch us with the awareness of your presence today. Send us the help we need.

---

23 January

Debbie came this morning and took me out for a while. It helped to have some company and a listening ear. I never thought that one day my daughter would be giving me relationship advice!

24 January

Joining the online service from church this morning when I got the news that my sister Jean has had a suspected heart attack. She's in hospital now, so I am waiting to hear further news. My soul was so troubled, but out of the blue I received a text invitation to chat if I needed to from a mature Christian friend with whom I have worked in the past. She was such a great help to me, so wise and understanding, a wonderful sounding board as I processed my disappointment and pain.

Once again God speaks to me through Lectio 365 *with these words:*

> *Today I rest in the blessing of mourning. I rest in the embrace of the Father of compassion and God of all comfort. I know that I can 'walk all the way into my sadness' and find your presence there.*[18]

We find ourselves mourning in all kinds of ways – for the loss of a loved one, in the breakdown of a relationship, after the shattering of a dream, when expectations remain unmet and so on. Sometimes it may be a combination of these. And God promises to comfort us in our sadness.

But my question today is: How to get that comfort into my troubled soul? When, like me, you live life through the lens of your emotions, your feelings can be all over the place and hard to control. Normally my sensitivity and ability to feel things is an asset, but when I lose my way, it is a liability big time. So how to receive the comfort of God?

Answers on a postcard (use a first-class stamp please, the mail is so slow these days).

25 January

I feel foolish and embarrassed about what has happened, as if I should have known better. No doubt many of my friends will be thinking that too, but I am assured by those to whom I look for counsel that I have no reason to feel stupid or to beat myself up. It happened, I am human, that's alright.

28 January

Better news today from my sister Jean. It wasn't a heart attack, but pain caused by prolonged use of certain medication, which has now been changed. Quite a relief.

The heartache I feel at the loss of a possible new relationship has been intense. I think it has triggered a grief reaction in me, a double loss – a second loss following the loss of Evelyn. I thought I was doing so well, but apparently not. I am at rock bottom, but at least my grief is coming out now. I'm sure that's for the best.

30 January

It is exactly six years ago today that my book Deep Calls to Deep *was published, based around the psalms of lament. It contains six wonderful stories of people who found that in the depths of their sorrow and sadness, God was there. I think I could write my own chapter now. In the introduction I wrote that the book will 'provide wisdom that we can store away for future reference, for no one knows what the future may bring. We may be standing on firm ground today, but tomorrow we may find ourselves overwhelmed by the waves and breakers.'*[19] *It seems that that day has come for me, and I need to find God in my own deep place right now.*

31 January
My grief journey is taking me to some tough places of late and requires a lot of soul-searching. A friend helpfully says, 'Keep doing the good albeit painful work. It will be worth its weight in gold.' So glad that Jesus is there for me no matter what. His mercy and grace are all I need. Oh, and a few good friends. I have been able to call on several for advice, prayer and a shoulder to cry on.

Finding strength in God

> When David and his men reached Ziklag, they found it destroyed by fire and their wives and sons and daughters taken captive. So David and his men wept aloud until they had no strength left to weep… David was greatly distressed because the men were talking of stoning him; each one was bitter in spirit because of his sons and daughters. But David found strength in the Lord his God.
> 1 SAMUEL 30:3–4, 6

The scene of devastation that greeted David and his men when they returned to their home base understandably triggered in them a massive grief reaction. They appeared to have lost everything – their homes burned to the ground, their belongings plundered and their families taken hostage. These hardened fighting men burst into tears and cried until they could cry no more.

It was good that they could express their emotions and feel their pain. Tears are not a sign of weakness, but of caring, and even grown men need to cry. Tears bring release and healing and are a natural and healthy response to loss. Soon, however, as the reality of what has happened sank in, their sadness turned to anger. Someone must be blamed, and that someone was David. They threatened to stone him.

David's distress was now multiplied, concern for his own life added to the sense of loss he felt over his family. How did he respond? In his crisis he consciously turned to God and sought to find the strength to cope through his faith. He made a deliberate choice not to turn away from God, but to turn towards God in his moment of need. He chose to step aside.

We know from the book of Psalms that this was a tried and tested strategy for David, and that his faith strengthened him through many trials. I imagine he prayed, and maybe shouted at God, then sang his praise and voiced his lament before eventually entrusting himself and his loved ones to God. Eugene Peterson brilliantly sums up what happened like this:

> David prayed; David worshipped; David called on his pastor Abiathar for counsel. David went deep within himself, met God, and found strength and direction to stride into the way of salvation. As his exterior world collapsed, he returned to the interior, rebuilt his primary identity, recovered his base.[20]

Having spoken with Abiathar, the priest, he came up with a plan of action which was successful. Not all stories have a happy ending, but this one did. The families were rescued and the goods restored.

Depression

The loss of a spouse is probably one of the most painful events any of us will ever experience, and it is not surprising that it creates in us a strong emotional response. It represents the loss of our companion and lover, as well as being the death of our imagined future and our hopes of what may have been. Justifiably we feel bereft.

The grief journey is often pictured as a U-shaped valley, and at our lowest point in the journey we are likely to feel depressed. We hit rock bottom emotionally, and perhaps mentally and spiritually. Our mood is low and we feel sad, sorrowful, lonely and pessimistic. There seems to be no hope, and we are filled with despair. We find concentration hard, lack motivation and have difficulty sleeping. We feel down on ourselves and can't see a way forward. Just getting through the day can feel like a triumph, which it is. These are all classic symptoms of depression.

However, to feel depressed is not the same as *being* depressed. In grief we may legitimately feel depressed for a short while, even acutely so, but it is not a permanent state, as in clinical depression. Normally, with the passing of time and some good self-care, our mood will lift and lighten, and we will feel hope rise again within us. This is not to minimise how dark some days may feel, but it is to recognise that we may experience some of the symptoms of depression without being in the grip of depression. We may be walking through the valley of deep darkness, but we are coming through, and that is the truth on which to rest. We remember the adage 'This too shall pass.' The clouds will lift, and the sun will shine again. As the psalmist said, 'Weeping may stay for the night, but rejoicing comes in the morning' (Psalm 30:5).

If we find we get stuck in a very low mood for a long period of time (several weeks) it is time to seek the help of a trusted counsellor, doctor or pastor. If we find we have stopped caring about our appearance, are not eating well, cannot function in daily life or are withdrawing ourselves from others, we must recognise these as danger signals and seek specialist help. There is no shame in this. It does not necessarily mean that we are ill or that we are inadequate in some way. It is simply part of our human condition, the vulnerability that comes with grief, and we are wise to admit our need of help.

FEBRUARY 2021

Struggling

Fix your eyes on Jesus

> And let us run with perseverance the race marked out for us,
> fixing our eyes on Jesus, the pioneer and perfecter of faith.
> HEBREWS 12:1–2

The great biblical antidote to the negative feelings created in us by the challenges of life is to fix our eyes on Jesus. It is to turn our thoughts towards him and, if we have lost connection with him through the difficulties we face, to consciously bring ourselves back into relationship with him.

When Peter took his eyes off Jesus he began to sink. When his eyes were on him, he could walk on water, but as soon as he looked at the wind and the waves, he began to sink (Matthew 14:29–30).

Hebrews tells us that a key aspect of perseverance is to deliberately fix our eyes on Jesus, the pioneer and perfecter of our faith. His example of endurance can inspire us to keep going, and as *The Message* puts it, 'will shoot adrenaline into your souls!' (Hebrews 12:3). We can find stamina to run the particular race marked out for us by turning to him.

There is no promise that our race will be easy or short. It is a marathon, and we need to summon up every ounce of strength, so we do not grow weary or lose heart.

To fix our eyes on Jesus is to make him the focus of our attention. We are not to look at ourselves, for there is no hope within us. We are not to look at our circumstances, for they may be hard and daunting and only make us despair. Neither are we to look to other people, for they cannot save us. We need to see Jesus, risen, ascended and glorified and to know that he is in control. 'At present we do not see everything subject to him [God]. But we do see Jesus, who was made lower than the angels for a little while, now crowned with glory and honour' (Hebrews 2:8–9). We are to consider him, that is think deeply about him, what he has accomplished and how he waits to help us today.

To fix our eyes on Jesus is to make him the object of our affection. We are to fall in love with him again and again. This is the essence of worship, and when we worship the focus will shift gradually from earth to heaven, from ourselves in our need to Jesus in his all-sufficiency. In difficult times we must return to our first love and engage with him not just in our minds but in our hearts as well.

Loneliness

The loss of a life partner will inevitably create a feeling of loneliness or isolation. When a relationship that gave comfort and strength to us over many years comes to an end we inevitably feel alone in the world. Even when we are surrounded by people, we may feel lonely inside, for a part of us is missing. David Kessler writes, 'You can be in a large group of friends and relatives and feel as disconnected as if you were lost in the desert.'[21] For some, bereavement means living alone after years of sharing a home with another person. We are bound to feel that loss, and even the most well-connected and gregarious will be affected.

Loneliness may be at its peak during long winter nights, weekends or even particular times of day. Eating alone can be a specific trial, as there may be no one to talk to and food never tastes as good when we eat alone. Who can we talk to when we want to comment on the news or respond to a TV programme? It is the absence of the other's presence that we are feeling when we are lonely. Feeling lonely after a major loss is normal and to be expected.

However, the downward drag of loneliness easily pulls us into isolation and unhealthy grieving. It takes courage and personal strength to push through the invisible barrier it creates between us and other people. Relationships are essential for our healing, so we must fight the temptation to hide away. We must find ways to interact with others – drop-in centres, church groups, clubs and societies are a good place to start. We can consider joining a grief support group. We can take the initiative to call friends and invite others into our life. Above all, we can choose to be proactive and take some risks.

1 February

The start of February, a new month. It must mean something in these dark and difficult days of lockdown when the weather is cold, the skies are grey and everyone feels miserable. I received a lovely gift of bulbs and seeds from a friend which reminds me that spring is on its way, and that there is some work in the garden to be done – and in my soul as well.

And also, after my request for 'answers on a postcard' (24 January), a book with the title <u>Postcards from the Land of Grief</u> arrived.[22] *Some people are just so thoughtful, aren't they? We must see in their kindness and thoughtfulness the very kindness and thoughtfulness of God and take heart. Even in the darkness there are glimpses of light if we choose to see them.*

4 February

It's a scene that was played out so many times during my marriage. I would be scratching around trying to find something, and Evelyn would ask in her gentle, Scottish accent, 'What have you lost?' The answer would usually be something like my pen, car keys or glasses. Then we would hunt together until the object was found.

Recently I lost my letter opener. Made of bamboo and decorated in tribal art forms, it wasn't valuable but full of sentimental attachment from our time in Borneo. Jenny, my cleaner, and I searched the house for it, but it has never been found. It is lost. My best guess is that it went in the bin along with envelopes that had been opened and were no longer needed. A sad end for a treasured object.

But 'What have you lost?' is a good question in these days of lockdown and restriction. All of us have lost something. Indeed, most of us have suffered multiple losses. We may be acutely aware of them or we may not yet have realised. We may be shielding ourselves from the reality of loss, because all loss involves grief, and grief is painful. Sometimes we press on regardless, choosing not to face the pain. But unfaced pain needs a place to go, and if we press it down inside of us it will stay there unresolved, waiting for its time to erupt.

It seems far better to face the pain of loss and to acknowledge our sadness. It takes courage, I know, but it is in these deep places where we meet God. Remember the words of Jesus, 'Blessed are those who mourn for they will be comforted' (Matthew 5:4). It can seem like an age before we feel any sense of healing, but with time it will come. We may weep for a 'night', but joy will come in the 'morning' (Psalm 30:5).

5 February

When talking recently about my own losses, I was asked, 'What would you say to someone you were mentoring in a similar position to yourself?' A good question. In reply, I said something like this:

1. *Be kind to yourself.*
2. *Remember you are only human and what you are feeling is perfectly normal.*
3. *Remember the words my mother used to say: 'This too shall pass.'*
4. *Ask for help. Who is there who will listen to you? Grief is a story that needs to be told, again and again. It is a burden that needs to be lightened, and the more we tell it, the lighter it becomes.*
5. *Have a good cry, often. Let the pain out. Don't be ashamed of tears, they are healing. Express your anger or frustration, especially with God. He can take it.*
6. *Find some strategies to help you through when the pain is acutest – for example, find friends to talk to when you are most lonely. Not for serious talk, but for fun and lightness and normality.*
7. *Keep a sense of perspective. Yes, it hurts like crazy at the moment, but it will get better. It is not the end of the world.*

Well, now to practise what I preach.

6 February

Just begun to reread The Land Between *by Jeff Manion, subtitled 'Finding God in difficult transitions'. When I read it before, I didn't really connect with it. This morning, however, it seems more relevant. I am particularly struck by this paragraph:*

I firmly believe that the Land Between – that space where we feel lost or lonely or deeply hurt – is fertile ground for our spiritual transformation and for God's grace to be revealed in magnificent ways. But in addition to being the bearer of mercy, I also have the privilege of challenging God's people to holiness, and while the Land Between is prime real estate for faith transformation, it is also the space where we can grow resentful, bitter, and caustic if our responses are unguarded. The wilderness where faith can thrive is the very desert where it can dry up and die if we are not watchful.[23]

Much to think about and ponder.

---

8 February

I really enjoy musical theatre, so last night's Musicals: The Greatest Show *on BBC1 was a real treat. One song stood out for me, a song I hadn't heard before, called 'You Will Be Found', from the Broadway hit* Dear Evan Hansen.

It's a song about loneliness and the feeling that no one notices you, that you are all alone. The message is simple – if you ask for help, someone will come by and befriend you. If you reach out your hand, help will come. No matter what struggles you are facing, despite how you may feel alone in the world, you're not alone. Someone will find you, remind you that you are not alone and help you through the dark times.

The presenter, Sheridan Smith, said she had been playing the song continuously since hearing it. Her own struggles in life are well documented, and I am sure many other people in these lockdown days found themselves resonating with the song. Perhaps it has too optimistic a view of human nature, though, for help does not always come so easily or quickly. But I know myself how powerful friendship can be when we are feeling lonely, and how ready so many are to reach out a helping hand when we admit our need.

What strikes me most is how songs can tap into the mood of the times, and how lyrics can reflect spiritual truth. This song reminds us surely of a God who came to seek and to save the lost, of Jesus the good shepherd who comes looking for us in our need. I love the story in John's gospel about the blind man who, having been healed, was cast out by the religious leaders. When Jesus heard this, he went and 'found him' (John 9:35). Remember the great gospel hymn 'Amazing Grace'? It has this line – 'I once was lost but now am found, was blind but now I see.' That's the heart of the gospel.

Today, whatever loneliness we face or whatever darkness stalks our souls, we have this glad assurance – that if we ask God for help, he will come and find us. 'This poor man called, and the Lord heard him; he saved him out of all his troubles' (Psalm 34:6).

9 February

Enjoyed a walk while it was snowing gently this afternoon. Really invigorating. This was followed by a nice coffee. I'm surprised how these simple things can lift my mood.

10 February

I'm enjoying working my way through The Land Between *by Jeff Manion and delighted that my ability to study has returned after an absence of several months. It is one of the ways I connect deeply with God and this book is helping me navigate the transition that follows bereavement, as painful and complicated as it has been. One of Manion's main points is that God led Israel into the wilderness so that they would learn to trust him and grow to know his faithfulness. Rather than grumble and complain, we can choose to trust God. It seems like a pertinent lesson for me.*

12 February

About ten days ago, on a visit to my local post office, I bought two packs of stamps. Nowadays this is an expensive purchase, about £20. A couple of days later, I remembered I had bought stamps and went to find them. But where were they? I knew I would have put them away safely, and my coat was the obvious place. I searched through every pocket twice, but to no avail. The next day I decided to look in my rucksack, which I had with me at the time. Again, I searched diligently but with the same negative outcome. I was feeling frustrated with myself by this time. Where could they be?

A week after the purchase, when I was again at the post office, I asked the postmaster if anyone had found and handed in two packs of stamps. Apparently not, although he did sympathise with me and acknowledged that people often leave things they have bought on the counter – but not my stamps. By now I was berating myself for this carelessness, as if I had lost the world. Do you ever do that? Turn in on yourself and doubt your own ability, question your own judgement?

Well, it has continued to nag away at me. I even searched the coat I was wearing yet again, without success. Then a simple thought entered my head. Perhaps I had put them in my wallet? Sure enough, they were there, in a place of safety. Now I am congratulating myself on such a great insight and thinking I am not so careless after all. My self-esteem has rocketed again. Oh, the joys of being only human!

13 February

I have no experience in looking after houseplants, and I certainly don't have green fingers. A little orchid appeared to be dead until a few weeks ago when buds started to appear. Now it has beautiful white and purple flowers. What an illustration of the power of nature, and what a message of hope to keep on believing when all seems lost.

14 February

I have never bothered at all about Valentine's Day. Evelyn and I did not send each other cards or exchange gifts, so generally speaking it passed me by. That is until this year, when I have noticed it more and with a degree of pain.

This morning's devotional from <u>Lectio 365</u> heightened my sense of loss with its focus on love. A prayer from Pete Greig was quoted which has this section:

> *Finally we ask you to look upon the elderly gentleman gazing today at a fading sepia photograph in a silver frame of a wedding at another time. Look at him and look with him and be with him in the remembering and the unremembering too.*[24]

No fading sepia photo for me to look at, but the tears begin to flow. I'm thinking about a love I had and lost; a love I almost had, but now is gone; and the hope I hold for a love that is yet to be. 'Lord, in your mercy, hear my prayer.'

Now on this sabbath day I enter my prayer space to offer myself again to God, although there is pain in this offering:

> *Take my love; my Lord I pour, At Thy feet its treasure-store;*
> *Take myself and I will be, Ever, only, all for Thee.*
> F.R. Havergal (1836–79)

19 February

Dearly loved and safely held.

20 February

Today I am leading the first of six online sessions based on my new book, <u>Mentoring Conversations</u>. It is for friends in Singapore and *promoted in partnership with The Discipleship Training Centre, which is based there. It is good to have a focus in these difficult days, and to know that God can still use me. Then this afternoon I will take my grandsons, George and Jacob, for a visit to the park and then back here for a while.*

21 February

Spoke this morning via Zoom to a church in Sheffield about my experiences over the past year. Afterwards one of the leaders remarked that it was 'pure gold', a comment that takes me back to the words given to me on 31 January. Perhaps good will come out of this struggle after all?

24 February

Had a conversation today with my good friend Scott Schaum, who lives in the US. He shared with me the principle that when we are in leadership, especially in caring for others pastorally, God often allows us to suffer things that will later be useful to us in our ministry of comfort and consolation. In the Psalms we read that God 'sent a man before them [Israel] – Joseph, sold as a slave' (Psalm 105:17). All the trials Joseph experienced were to prepare him to give help to his family later, during the famine. In the economy of God, nothing is wasted. Perhaps God is preparing me now through my own struggles for the work he has in mind for me.

28 February

I am joining tonight an online retreat led by Sharon Garlough Brown, the author of <u>Sensible Shoes</u>, a wonderful book about the spiritual journey of four ladies who meet during a retreat and become firm friends.[25] *In story form it teaches many profound truths about spiritual formation and how God works in us to shape us into the likeness of Christ. I am really looking forward to learning from her.*

Tested

> Consider it pure joy, my brothers and sisters, whenever you face trials of many kinds, because you know that the testing of your faith produces perseverance. Let perseverance finish its work so that you may be mature and complete, not lacking anything.
> JAMES 1:2–4

I love cricket, and one form of the international game is played between two teams over five days. It is called a test match for the simple reason that such a long game tests the physical strength, depth of character and sporting ability of those who take part.

Many of the trials of life that come our way test our character and faith. They search us out and show what we are made of, whether or not our faith is strong enough to endure hardship and pain. Sometimes we are found wanting and are tempted to give up; other times we surprise ourselves by the strength we find to go on.

There is no doubt that bereavement presents us with a test of both our character and our faith. The loss we experience and the pain we endure require us to call on our inner resources. Often such suffering draws us closer to God because we know we cannot get by in our own strength. We have to turn to God for his help, and our faith is deepened as a result. Dependency is a wonderful by-product of grief.

Not only that, but by facing our pain and not giving up we develop perseverance, a word which could easily be translated as 'resilience'. It is a word which describes the long-distance runner who presses on through the pain barrier to finish the race, and it is a mark of personal and spiritual maturity. We would not choose to experience such difficulties in order to grow, but character growth is only possible when we face trials and testings and, with God's help, come through.

Bereavement as transition

During the past month I have been looking again at my notes on transition and change in readiness for an online course I will be leading in April. Although I have never read this elsewhere, it seems to me that bereavement leads us into a major time of transition. The principles I have taught many times about navigating transition can be applied to the grief journey. A key thought is this: all transition involves change, and change involves loss, and therefore grief.

Basically, the process is this:

1. We are in a settled situation, where we feel at home and comfortable.
2. Something happens to change the status quo, and we enter a period of feeling unsettled or destabilised.
3. This is followed by a period of chaos as we try to come to terms with what has happened.
4. Gradually we learn to adapt to the new situation and we begin to resettle.
5. Finally, we arrive at a place where we feel at home again and are comfortable with the new normal.

Transition can be described as the period from when we are first aware of the need to change, to the time when the new situation is established. This can take anything from six months to two years, which fits well with estimates of the grief journey.

It is important to recognise that such a transition involves a disruption to our way of life, which requires us in turn to make new behavioural responses. It is as if the pieces of the jigsaw that make up our life are thrown into the air and we have to wait for them to come down again before we can re-assemble them into a new pattern. Again, it is easy to see the connection with the disruption to life caused by the death of a spouse and the adjustment that is necessary.

What is helpful is to recognise there is a pattern and shape to transition, and although it takes time, we will make it through.

MARCH 2021

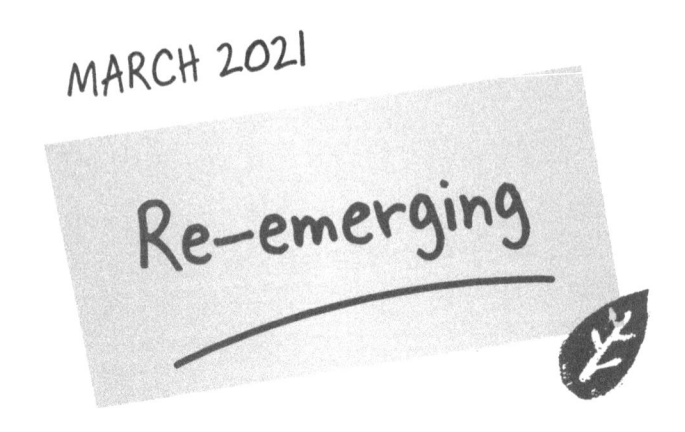

Re-emerging

Not left alone

> 'If you love me, keep my commands. And I will ask the Father, and he will give you another advocate to help you and be with you forever – the Spirit of truth. The world cannot accept him, because it neither sees him nor knows him. But you know him, for he lives with you and will be in you. I will not leave you as orphans; I will come to you.'
> JOHN 14:15–18

In the upper room, Jesus tells his disciples that he will soon return to the Father. His departure will be to them like a bereavement, for they had been so attached to him. But his promise is that they will not be left alone like orphans. He will come to them through his Spirit, and they will continue to know his presence within them. They may feel bereft, but that feeling will be temporary.

This promise of Jesus was fulfilled on the day of Pentecost, when the Spirit was given to the church for the very first time. Since then all believers have the Holy Spirit within them. He is our advocate or, as other translations put it, our comforter. The Greek word used here means literally 'the one who draws alongside', suggesting a helper in our time of need.

When we lose our spouse, we may indeed feel that we are bereft, as if the most important person in the world has been taken from us. We may feel as lonely as an orphan, because there is now no one to care for us. We feel empty and vulnerable. Yet we are not without hope or without the power to pull through. The Holy Spirit is there with us, not only healing our hurt and comforting us in our sadness but empowering us to live again.

I remember when my car broke down at the side of a busy motorway. I felt alone and at risk, so I called for help. Very quickly a patrolman from the breakdown organisation I belong to was on the scene to rescue me. He literally drew up alongside me, sorted out the problem and got me on the road again.

Jesus has given us the Holy Spirit to do just that for us in our times of bereavement and loss. Not only will he come to comfort us, but he will give us the motivation to start living again and to adjust to life without our loved one.

Identity

When we are married, especially over a long period of time, our identity is inevitably tied to that of our spouse. We are seen as a couple. Other people cannot think of one of us without thinking of the other. For example, our friends tell me that they always thought of us as 'TonyandEv'. It is probably the way that we felt as well, a reflection of the biblical statement that in marriage the two become one (Genesis 2:24; Matthew 19:6). Over the years our separate identities have been merged into one. We were a pair, and our lives were intertwined.

However, it is also a reminder that when one partner dies that joint identity is lost and we have to find a new identity. 'Who am I now?' is a question often asked by those who are bereaved. It is a fundamental question, too, striking at the very core of our being.

Our status has changed, and people see us differently. In my case I am now a widower, and frankly I don't like the sound of that. It feels a bit sad, and I fear people will look at me with pity. I am also single again, which affects how I feel about myself and how others of the opposite sex regard me. I am 'available' again and have to relearn how to relate again on this basis, which makes me nervous. Furthermore, I am no longer a husband with someone to love and care for. Where will my capacity to love find its expression now?

What has not changed, though, is my relationship to God. I am still his deeply loved child. My worth and value, my security and confidence, are found in knowing that I am loved unconditionally and for all time. But I may have to find that place in God again. I will have to rediscover that sense of being God's beloved child in the midst of my pain and loss, my emotional instability and my inability to focus my thoughts. That may take time and some effort on my part, but God's attitude towards me has not changed one iota. I am, and always will be, his much-loved child. That is a given.

---

1 March

Today has been crammed with God, and not because I expected it or felt more spiritual than normal – quite the reverse in fact. But as I look back on it now, I am amazed at how my little life has touched the lives of others around the world.

It started with an early morning call to a senior mission leader overseas in need of pastoral support, and we connected deeply as we spoke. Then a helpful dialogue with a friend about transition and how God works in us through times of change. After lunch an invigorating walk in the countryside with a pastor on sabbatical, talking about the things of God and hopefully encouraging him as he moves forward in the vision that God has given him. A brief visit to see my daughter on the way back to return a special Lego figure that grandson George had left behind. Then a quick shop at my favourite supermarket on the way home and a friendly conversation with the lady on duty at the coffee counter.

When I got home, I checked my emails and there was a lovely response from a couple in the US who had been reading Finding Refuge, *the story of the last months of Evelyn's life. The woman had been reading it to her husband in the evenings and they had laughed and cried as they read. This is such an affirmation for me, since her role is in the media and involves recording stories of what God is doing.*

I cried as I took it all in. How come one day is filled to overflowing with God, and another I feel he is nowhere to be seen?

But the thing that cheered me the most was what happened on the walk this afternoon. We were so engrossed in our conversation that we got lost and were miles from where we had parked the car. As we realised this, a woman came out of a nearby farm. We asked her where we were and how we could get back to our cars. Knowing it was a long way, she offered to give us a lift, then realised her car was packed with all kinds of paraphernalia (she had been to feed her horse). She was very embarrassed at the state of her car and full of apologies, but we managed to squeeze in – quite a feat given that my friend is 6'3" and I am 6'2". But beggars can't be choosers and we were so grateful for the lift because we were indeed a long way from where we needed to be.

Truly a good Samaritan, and we told her so.

2 March
After lamenting the difficulty of eating alone, some friends offered

to share a Zoom lunch with me today. It was great to chat to Ben and Kat over my soup.

Then this evening a Zoom call with Arne, a Norwegian friend with whom I have shared the leading of many training courses over the years. Sadly, Arne's wife was killed in a road traffic accident just a few months after Evelyn died. We are of a similar age, and here we are both grieving for our companions. Arne's loss seems more difficult than mine – so sudden, so tragic and no time to say goodbye or to prepare oneself. Fortunately, Arne is surrounded by a loving and caring family. We laughed together as we shared stories of learning to cook for ourselves. It seems Arne lives on fishcakes!

---

5 March

Once more <u>Lectio 365</u> seems to be right on the mark for me today. I think Pete Greig and his team are writing with me in mind! This week's theme has been about coming to terms with unanswered prayer. How do we avoid allowing disappointment to crush our hopes, rob us of our joy and undermine our faith in God? The answer according to 1 Thessalonians 5:16–18 is to keep rejoicing in all circumstances and finding reasons to give thanks to God, even in the small things of life.

Carla Harding comments:

> *Giving thanks in all circumstances isn't the same as giving thanks for all circumstances. Paul isn't extending an invitation to delusion or commanding me to bury my head in the sand. He's encouraging me to notice and celebrate the best in my life, even in the midst of the worst. Giving thanks helps me to see beyond the prison walls of my present worries and struggles, to glimpse the hope-filled horizon beyond.*[26]

What can we find to rejoice in today? Where do we notice God's goodness in our life?

6 March

Something unusual happened today when I stepped out of the house to walk across to my office. It was a bright, sunny morning and as the light hit me, I felt something lift inside me. It's hard to explain, but I felt different, and it was the light that made the difference. I am not aware that I have ever been affected by seasonal affective disorder, but perhaps this year, with its dark, cold and murky days, has affected me in addition to my grief and the intensity of lockdown. Certainly, the brighter days have cheered me up, and there is more to come as we look forward to spring.

7 March

Leading a retreat based on the book of Ruth over the next three days for a small group who are on the staff of a large church in Singapore, but who feel the need for silence and solitude. We will seek to answer some of these questions that emerge from the story:

- *Does God have a plan for my life, and is it working?*
- *How am I to respond to setbacks, disappointments and heartbreak?*
- *Can I trust God with my future?*
- *Is God's will really the best?*
- *Is my life at the mercy of chance or is there a divine purpose at work?*

One commentator writes:

> *If there is one theme more than any other which dominates the book of Ruth, it is that of the over-ruling providence of God, and our human dependence on him... Providence says that God is there, God cares, God rules, and God provides. Faith in such a God undergirds every chapter of Ruth.*[27]

8 March

Last night a friend shared with me some words from Isaiah which he felt were for my situation:

> *Arise, shine for your light has come,*
>   *and the glory of the Lord rises upon you.*
> *See, darkness covers the earth*
>   *and thick darkness is over the peoples,*
> *but the Lord rises upon you*
>   *and his glory appears over you.*
> ISAIAH 60:1–2

Certainly, the darkness of winter lockdown has been mirrored in my own soul at times, but this morning I was up very early for a Zoom call to Singapore, and as I came out of the house into the office, I noticed the sun appearing tentatively despite the clouds. It caught my attention and gave me the sense of a new day dawning.

Then in my teaching on the book of Ruth, I see that I have called the final session, 'A new day dawns', based on chapter 4. Naomi and Ruth had seen some dark days, but for them also the sun of righteousness had risen 'with healing in its rays' (Malachi 4:2).

May all who have suffered loss, faced disappointment or known pain or suffering in these pandemic days be blessed today with a new God-given sense of hope and optimism.

12 March

Meeting my friend Cliff for a walk this morning, something we are allowed to do in this season of lockdown. Walking has meant so much to me at this time, being good for my physical and mental health, and I try to walk every day, even if it is by myself. It is such an apt metaphor for the grief journey and for the Christian life in general. Meeting up with a friend is even more helpful, though, and we are able to chat freely and deeply, a release for us both. I am blessed with so many friends who offer me this kind of support. I think 'walking and talking' is a ministry in its own right.

---

14 March
Awake early today, although I slept well. Today is a double whammy as far as grief is concerned – today is Mother's Day, tomorrow my birthday. Both events bring home my sense of loss now that Evelyn is gone.

Evelyn was a real mother, to me as well as the children! She loved to care and showed her love by her actions, looking after us, keeping the home going, making sure we were fed and watered. Today we will visit her grave and lay flowers. I don't really like to go there, to be honest. It is a cold, brutal place in some ways, and yet the place where her body lies buried. I know she is in heaven, of course, and free from her suffering and pain, but the grave reminds me starkly that she is gone.

Then Monday will be my first birthday without her. I have lots of cards and presents to open, but how strange it will be to do so alone. No one there to whom to say, 'What a beautiful card, what kind words, what lovely handwriting.' No one with whom to share a bottle of wine, a box of chocolates or a new book.

It often feels like I live in two worlds at the same time. The one universe is full of kind, compassionate friends doing their best to comfort me and reassure me. I so appreciate them, and I enjoy that world. But then there is the space within my head, a parallel universe, to which I must return. That world is empty, just me there, alone with my thoughts and my brooding. Good Christian that I am, I know I am not alone, but I could still do with a birthday kiss, a loving smile, a glance that says, 'I'm here for you.'

I don't write to elicit sympathy. I write to express my feelings.

Writing is cathartic – it helps me organise my thoughts and bring some order to my emotions. I will feel better after this. I hope you understand. This Mother's Day will be a sad one for many people. Grief is one thing we have in common.

15 March

Enjoyed a Zoom birthday celebration with friends online. Lots of fun and laughter, just what is needed. It is hard not to think of last year's special celebration – my 70th, and the last time Evelyn would see most of her friends and our son Alistair and his family, who travelled over from Australia especially to be with us.

19 March

Spoke by Zoom to a group of expatriate believers in the Middle East first thing today. What new and amazing doors have opened for us! It is good to have these ministry opportunities again. I'm sure it is part of the healing process for me.

20 March

One thing I have been doing over the last few weeks is to invite friends for a chat via Zoom, a defence against my loneliness. Evenings are the worst time for me, and Saturday evening the hardest of all. I have been pleasantly surprised by the willingness of everyone I invited to connect with me. Perhaps they are lonely too during lockdown? It felt like a big risk at first, fearing rejection, but it was something I felt I could do to help myself through this period, and it has worked.

21 March

The Sunday evening online retreat with Sharon Garlough Brown from the US has been a wonderful resource for me. I have enjoyed her teaching so much and the practical application in helping us to listen to God for ourselves. It has rekindled my love of leading retreats and awakened my desire to continue in this ministry going forwards.

24 March

Another great opportunity today, teaching about resilience with a group of missionaries and church leaders in Northern Ireland. I am sharing the day with Debbie Duncan, a health professional who has also written about this topic. We seem to get on, and I think the day should go well.

31 March

I have not done any 'proper' cooking for a while, and with no one to teach me anything new, I feel my skills have plateaued – indeed, they may even have declined as I can no longer remember how to do some of the dishes I was taught early on. So, I am looking forward to the day when friends can not only visit the garden, but also the kitchen!

And the busyness of life recently has meant that I have had to be content with survival cooking. I am still using the oven, and burning my fingers occasionally, but mostly to warm things up or cook simple things like baked potato or sausages. But I am eating well. And there is always my dear friend, Mrs Microwave.

Today I have the slow cooker on, the first time for a while. It seems the safest way to cook, and it gives me three or four meals at a time, so always something for the freezer as well. And the quality is good too. But the cookery book feels a long way off at the moment, which will disappoint many of you. Instead, I may write something on my grief journey. There might even be a chapter on 'How to boil an egg.'

Grief turned to joy

> Very truly I tell you, you will weep and mourn while the world rejoices. You will grieve, but your grief will turn to joy. A woman giving birth to a child has pain because her time has come; but when her baby is born she forgets the anguish because of her joy that a child is born into the world. So with you: now is your time of grief, but I will see you again and you will rejoice, and no one will take away your joy.
> JOHN 16:20–22

Once again in the upper room, Jesus takes time to encourage his disciples. Although his death will be an occasion of much sadness and grief for them, it will not be the end of the story. The implication is that they will see him again because he will rise from the dead. The resurrection will be the source of much joy for them, and even though he will then return to heaven, this internalised joy will not be taken away from them.

Joy is an unmistakable mark of the kingdom of God, and it cannot be suppressed for long. Even grief has its season, and the time of sadness will pass. Yes, there will be a time of anguish, of tears and sorrow, but this need not be a permanent state. Those who have given birth know how the pain of childbirth is quickly evaporated by the appearance of the newborn. We can dare to believe that one day the clouds of our sorrow will part and the sun will shine again.

We have the consolation that one day we will be re-united with our loved ones in heaven, but that does not mean we cannot know happiness or joy until then. Once our emotions settle, we will feel our joy returning, for it is an expression of the life of God within us, and that life is indestructible. We must not be afraid to feel joy again, to laugh and have fun. It is what our loved one would wish for us, and it is a sign that the Spirit is at work in us, for the joy of the Lord is our strength (Nehemiah 8:10).

Letting go

We have seen already that bereavement is a form of transition, and to make a successful transition we must let go of the past in order to take hold of the present and the future. Letting go is never easy, but letting go is not the same as forgetting or no longer loving. It is the realisation that if we cling to the past we will never be able to move forward in life. We run the risk of being marooned in our grief, castaway on an island of sadness.

This is surely not what our loved one would wish for us. When Mary met the risen Jesus in the garden her initial response was to hold on to him as tightly as possible, but Jesus carefully reminded her that this was not the best way forward. 'Do not hold on to me,' he said, 'for I have not yet ascended to the Father' (John 20:17).

The grieving process has been described as a journey of separation. In the early stages it is only natural that we should want to hold on to our loved one, thinking of them all the time and trying to keep the relationship alive. Gradually, however, as the weeks go by, we must live less in the past and find our feet in the present, coming to terms with the reality that our loved one has gone and will not return. Then, eventually, we will begin to accept the wisdom and necessity of not clinging to what once was, and we will find the courage to leave the grief of our loss behind us. We will see the importance of being truly present to the loved ones who are still with us, and the need to take hold of the new opportunities ahead of us.

We may fear that this is a form of betrayal, of being disloyal and disrespectful to our loved one. It is not. We will continue to love them and hold their memory close to our hearts. We will never forget them, but for the sake of our own health and well-being, and for the sake of those around us, it is necessary to let go.

APRIL 2021

Reconnecting

Grief at Easter (1)

> As the soldiers led [Jesus] away, they seized Simon from Cyrene, who was on his way to the country, and put the cross on him and made him carry it behind Jesus. A large number of people followed him, including women who mourned and wailed for him.
> LUKE 23:26–27

It may be because I am recently bereaved myself, but I have noticed more than ever before the note of honest grief in the Easter story. The death of Christ affected those around him deeply, as does the death of any loved one. Grief has a ripple effect. The gospel accounts give us permission to own and recognise our personal sense of loss, whatever form it takes.

To lose a child is perhaps the most painful type of bereavement, even when that child is an adult. To lose someone to violent and unjustified death, with public humiliation, intensifies a pain that already seems unbearable. How did Mary the mother of Jesus feel on that day as the sword of grief pierced her heart, just as Simeon had foretold (Luke 2:35)?

And what of the women who had followed him from Galilee, bravely gathered around the cross (Mark 15:40–41)? How painful it is to see a loved one suffer and pass through the stages of dying before your eyes, until they breathe their very last breath. Grief is part of loving. Those who love much, grieve much, although grief expresses itself in many ways. These women cared deeply for Jesus, had shared their resources with him and tenderly cared for him and his disciples practically. They did not back away from the pain of watching him die. They had to be there with him, but what anguish they must have felt.

Think of the disciples too, those men who had left all to follow him, pinned their hopes on him, loved him as a brother and friend. Most could not bear to watch him die and hid themselves away. How often we want to pretend that death has not happened, that it's just a dream, until reality strikes home. Things will never be the same again. Some of our dreams will not come to pass, and the future we imagined is now impossible. No wonder some fell into despair, like the two on the road to Emmaus. Downcast and dejected, they voice their misery: 'We had hoped that he was the one who was going to redeem Israel' (Luke 24:21). Depression is often an unwelcome visitor when we grieve.

For some, the death of a loved one awakens love within them and stimulates them to action. Nicodemus and Joseph of Arimathea go and gather the body, lovingly prepare it for burial and then place it in a garden tomb (John 19:38–42). At least they could do something tangible to express their love, and it helps. Sitting around moping can make matters worse. Doing something practical somehow helps assuage the anguish we feel.

Here are ordinary people, with human emotions like our own, dealing in the best way they can with the tragedy that has befallen them. But what the Easter story tells us is that we are never alone in our grief. Friends and family offer comfort and support, but most importantly God is with us. He knows grief too, for Jesus is the Son of God. The Father feels our pain and weeps with us in our loss.

Resilient grieving

Lucy Hone is a researcher in resilience based in New Zealand who has known intense grief. Her daughter Abi was killed in a car accident along with her best friend and her friend's mother. Her world was turned upside down by this tragic event. She went through all the normal reactions to loss (mostly numbness), but as she and her family sought to come to terms with what had happened, she began to consider if what she understood about resilience could help them cope with their grief. She didn't want simply to sit back and allow grief to overwhelm her but sought to proactively participate in the grieving process.

Her book *Resilient Grieving* outlines what we may do to enable the process of healthy grieving.[28] Normally the focus is on what people who are mourning may experience, and the emphasis is on the fact that grief is individual and that healing takes as long as it takes. This, she argues, actually encourages a passive approach, which is contrary to what we know about resilience. There are things we can do to assist the process of healthy grieving.

To adopt a more proactive approach is not to move into denial or to seek to accelerate the grieving process, but to recognise that we do have choice in the way we grieve. Rather than focus simply on the symptoms of grief, we can also learn strategies to help us weather the storm and, hopefully, adjust to our loss, return to functioning normally and start being productive again.

Being an active participant in the grieving process will aid our recovery. Rather than allowing ourselves to be overwhelmed, we can choose to put in place those behaviours and responses that will strengthen us physically and emotionally. Among these active coping mechanisms, we might consider finding strength through sharing with others, guarding the way we think, looking after our physical wellbeing, finding activities that help us to switch off and relax, cultivating positive emotions and seeking the help that comes from God.

2 April
Today is Good Friday, and we remember the death of Jesus on the cross. It reminds me that God the Father knows the pain of loss in his own heart and can therefore identify with those who grieve today. Anyone who has had the pain of seeing a loved one pass away before their very eyes will know how the women felt as they watched from a distance as Jesus hung on the cross.

3 April
Easter Saturday is often called Silent Saturday because it is the day between the death and the resurrection of Jesus. It reminds us of the times of darkness in our own lives, of periods of long waiting when nothing much seems to happen. Sometimes all we can do is wait for the darkness to pass and believe that joy will come in the morning.

4 April
Easter Sunday, and the victory of the resurrection. Sin has been dealt with, Satan has been defeated and death has been vanquished. These great realities comfort me deeply today, both in the sense that Evelyn's death was not the end for her, and also in that there is hope for me as I begin to look forward again. I feel a change inside me, as if I am daring to hope again, as if hope is rising within me. I am becoming more optimistic.

7 April

I shared with Debbie Hawker this morning my growing sense of optimism as I look to the future, and in particular how the vision of what God wants me to do in the next phase of my life is becoming clearer. It has all to do with the 'spacious' place of Psalm 18:19 – 'He brought me out into a spacious place; he rescued me because he delighted in me.' This is my story in a nutshell, past, present and future. He rescued me in the sense that I recovered from Covid. He takes delight in me because I am his deeply loved child. And looking ahead, the spacious place is where he wants to bring me – a place of freedom of movement where there is room to breathe, a place that is not overcrowded or cramped, a place which reflects the joy and goodness of the promised land.

What I see is that my main calling now will be in writing. My publisher BRF is keen for me to write more, and their invitation to make suggestions of what I want to write going forward seems to confirm this should be a priority for me. Writing is something I can do at my own pace and easily fits around other things.

Second, through attending the online Sacred Journey retreat with Sharon Garlough Brown, my love for leading retreats has been rekindled and in particular my passion to care for mission partners. This may be perhaps four times a year, but it gives me the opportunity to meet wonderful people, often in beautiful surroundings and sometimes to travel.

Third – and this is where the word 'spacious' really comes in – I want to leave time and room for the spontaneous, to be free to travel and be with people, visiting friends who mean something to me. This too, I believe, will be ministry but of an informal kind as we chat and share stories.

Debbie Hawker reminded me that a spacious place is the exact opposite of what I experienced when I was in intensive care with

Covid-19. There I couldn't breathe, was confined to bed and very much alone. This brought tears to my eyes. How marvellous God is! Truly he has delivered me because he delights in me!

8 April
Having shared yesterday with Debbie Hawker about my vision for the future, this morning's devotion from <u>Lectio 365</u> seemed more than just a little appropriate and confirmatory. Reflecting on John 21:3–7 and the appearance of the risen Jesus to the disciples who were fishing in Galilee, we were reminded that Jesus was bringing them back to their initial calling. We were then asked to ponder these questions: 'Do I feel caught between my calling and my immediate reality? Do I know what God wants me to do with my life?'[29]

Then there is a prayer, which I gladly made my own: 'Lord, remind me today of the commission you have given me, and help me to live a life worthy of the calling I have received (Ephesians 4:1).'

But the closing prayer is the one I want to offer today, in the light of my sharing yesterday and the growing sense of calling that I have:

> Lord, I am so thankful that you have spoken over me a commission, a unique calling to serve You and labour alongside You in the building of Your kingdom. I receive the commission afresh today. It feels too big for me – but in faith I receive it and commit once again to following you to the ends of the earth.

12 April
Today I am leading an online training course called New Directions, which is for mission partners returning to live in Britain after their time overseas. It's all about transition from one phase of life to another, and the change and loss that accompanies such a major upheaval.

I have taught this course many times in the past, but not for a number of years. When I started looking at the topic again some weeks ago, I was surprised by how relevant it is to me now. I hadn't realised that losing a spouse, or any form of bereavement, plunges one into a life transition.

Transition involves a major disruption to the structure of our life and adjusting to this requires us to behave in new ways. That certainly seems right, for my old way of living has gone and slowly I am rebuilding my life again.

16 April

Yesterday was a very hard day. Perhaps the best word is 'frustrating', because a lot of the things I had planned did not come to pass. I recorded a talk for a church to be used on Sunday, but then could not find the way to forward it to them. I spent ages trying to upload it, without success. Then my dental appointment for next week was cancelled after I had carefully arranged my schedule to make room for it. The gas engineer also cancelled (a problem with the boiler), and some friends who were coming today texted to apologise for not coming because something urgent had come up.

But there was more to my plummeting mood than just frustration. It has been a beautiful spell of weather, and I really fancied a walk in the countryside, but I have no one to go with at short notice. If Evelyn were here, we would take a drive and sit and enjoy a picnic in a beautiful spot somewhere. But she isn't here, so this is just another reminder of the loss of companionship and the loneliness that can follow even when you are doing well.

17 April

Like many people, I will be tuning in today to watch the funeral of Prince Philip. I'm sure it will touch many people in this year of grief, myself included. But I am a bit concerned by the description of the

Queen approaching it with 'quiet dignity'. It is not easy to grieve in public, and the world's media will be trained on her. She is both Queen and widow, grieving the loss of her soulmate of 73 years. I do hope in private that she can forget all about 'quiet dignity' and will be able to grieve with tears and feeling at the enormity of her loss. I saw a beautiful picture of them in their 'happy place', sitting together on the grass in the Scottish Highlands. It touches me deeply. It is this kind of connection that you lose when you lose a life partner. This is what accounts for the emptiness that is part of grief. The Queen will surely feel this, and rightly so.

18 April

I'm beginning to realise just how important contentment is in the process of transition. When the pattern of our life is changing, and we are moving from one phase to another, everything feels 'up in the air' and we are impatient for things to settle down again. But it takes time for life to recover its shape after loss or bereavement, and it can't be rushed.

In particular, I need to find contentment in being single, which I have to confess I am not finding easy. I do not enjoy the state of being 'unattached'. This morning I woke with the familiar words of Jesus in my mind, 'But seek first his kingdom and his righteousness, and all these things will be given to you as well' (Matthew 6:33). In other words, keep your eyes fixed on what God wants you to do at this moment and leave the rest to him. Things will happen in his good time.

As I pondered this, another verse came to mind, which I had used in the New Directions retreat last week:

> *For the Lord God is a sun and shield;*
>   *the Lord bestows favour and honour;*
> *no good thing does he withhold*
>   *from those whose way of life is blameless.*
> PSALM 84:11

Here we are reminded of the goodness of God. He does not hold anything back from us that in his wisdom and love can be considered to be good for us. So, if that thing that I so desperately want will be for my benefit and blessing, he will provide it for me in his good time. Meanwhile I am called to trust him during the waiting period and to rest contentedly in that knowledge.

---

19 April

Are you content? I have to confess that I am not always content with my lot, and after speaking last week on the New Directions course about this topic, my words have come back to bite me.

If I believe in the goodness of God (which I do) and if I know that God is loving and wise (which he is), I can trust him with the details of my life, both great and small. That 'thing' I so desire and feel I must have must be given over to him, surrendered to his love, so that he can decide if it is good for me or not.

Instead of stamping my feet like a naughty child denied a chocolate bar in the supermarket by a wise parent, I am called to be mature enough to submit my demandingness to God and allow him to direct my paths. I am to keep my eyes on the path ahead of me, walking as truly as I can in his ways and believing that in his perfect time he will do that which is best for me. I can trust that he will not withhold anything that is good from me, for he is not spiteful or mean.

If he does withhold something, it is because he knows it will not benefit me in the long run. He is both my sun (the source of joy) and my shield (protecting me from folly). When he withholds, however, he also bestows, and favour and honour accompany those who seek first his kingdom. If there is loss, there will be a compensatory gain.

With this mindset and his grace, I can learn contentment in his ordering of my life. Is that easy? No, definitely not. But it is what I aspire to today.

---

21 April

I've just been making arrangements for Evelyn's headstone. Local cemetery rules say that you have to wait at least six months before erecting a headstone to allow time for the ground to settle. Now that spring is here, it is a good time to set the ball rolling for what is still a fundamental part of saying farewell to her. It feels like her burial will not be complete until the grave is sorted.

It's a strange business, too, choosing a headstone from a catalogue with a whole range of styles and shapes, some simple and basic, some grand and ornate. What criteria do we use to decide? In the end I know that Evelyn would not want anything too fancy but would be comfortable with plain and simple, and that suits me as well. In the end I opt for the 'Ealing' in black granite, and also let them know the words to be engraved in gold lettering:

> *In loving memory of*
> *Evelyn Mary Horsfall*
> *1947–2020*
> *A much loved*
> *Wife, mother, grandma, sister, friend*
> *'To live is Christ, to die is gain'*

It will be a couple of months before it is erected, but it's a very earthy and solid reminder that she has really gone.

Grief at Easter (2)

> Now Mary stood outside the tomb crying. As she wept, she bent over to look in the tomb and saw two angels in white, seated where Jesus' body had been, one at the head and the other at the foot.
> JOHN 20:11–12

There is no day in the Christian calendar like Easter Sunday morning! The sense of joy and victory at the resurrection of Jesus never fails to excite me or to stir me to greater things in God. I am so sad that we cannot be together this year to sing those triumphant Easter hymns with our customary gusto and vigour. For those first disciples, however, the first day of the week did not begin with joy but with sadness, for they had no expectation or realisation that death had been defeated.

I find the story of Mary's visit to the tomb deeply moving in its simplicity and realism. Mary comes to the tomb, and she is crying. Tears are perhaps the most common expression of grief and loss, although not all express their sorrow through crying. But Mary does, without inhibition. Tears are healing and a way of releasing our emotions, so we have no need to feel embarrassed by our tears or feel the need to stifle them in public. Let the tears flow!

Mary's fear is that someone has stolen the body and dumped it somewhere else. That very thought grieves her deeply, and she is so caught up in her sadness that she does not recognise the risen Jesus standing nearby. Only when he speaks her name does the reality dawn on her, and she realises he is alive. Quickly she returns to the other disciples to tell them the joyful news: 'I have seen the Lord!', she declares (John 20:18).

We never get over our grief, but we do pass through it, and there will come a day when joy returns and we can live again. It may take time, and longer than we think, but eventually the scripture will come true for us and God will give us 'beauty instead of ashes, the oil of joy instead of mourning, and a garment of praise instead of a spirit of despair' (Isaiah 61:3).

Positive emotions

Research shows that people who cultivate positive emotions are more resilient in life and also in grieving.[30]

Negative emotions, such as sadness, despair, hopelessness, disappointment and anger, are natural during times of loss and need to be owned and acknowledged, but they need not be totally dominant. Even in times of difficulty we can still have positive emotions, which can help us pull through by enabling us to break free from the struggles we are facing, regain perspective, find extra strength and become more creative in finding solutions.

In fact, mourning has been described as an oscillation between sadness and other more positive emotions. Experiencing positive emotions is not a sign of denial, but a God-given way of coping and not being overwhelmed.

Positive emotions tend to be more fleeting than negative ones and less intense, so we can easily overlook them or undervalue them. This means that when they come along we are to savour them, to enjoy the moment of lightness and relief, and thereby gain full benefit. Resilient people give themselves permission to be human, to experience the full gamut of human emotions, both positive and negative. They choose not to be stuck in the darkness.

What are the positive emotions? We can suggest things like satisfaction in achievements, awe at the beauty and wonders of creation, hope in the sense of optimism and faith, being inspired and comforted by the example and encouragement of others, gratitude for what we do have, peace and calmness, humour and laughter, and allowing ourselves to both give and receive love.

Most of us are hardwired to focus on the negative and to allow negative emotions to dominate us. It takes effort to notice the moments of oscillation to better things when our mood lifts, our joy returns or we suddenly feel lighter in ourselves. These are God-given markers of his presence even in the darkest hour, to be celebrated and enjoyed.

MAY 2021

Re-envisioning

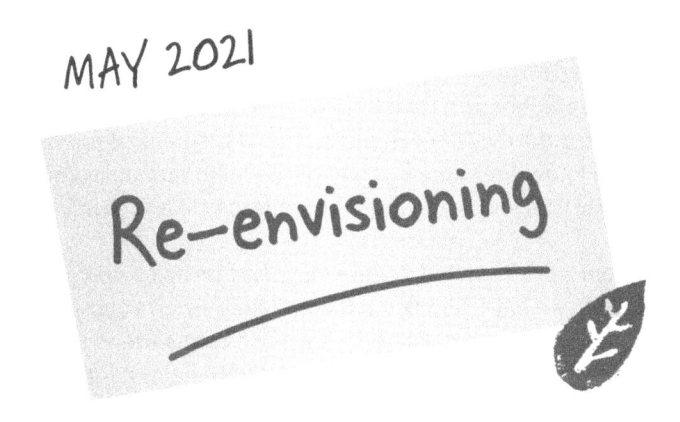

The power of friendship

> Two are better than one,
>   because they have a good return for their labour;
> if either of them falls down,
>   one can help the other up.
> But pity anyone who falls
>   and has no one to help them up.
> Also, if two lie down together, they will keep warm.
>   But how can one keep warm alone?
> Though one may be overpowered,
>   two can defend themselves.
> A cord of three strands is not quickly broken.
> ECCLESIASTES 4:9–12

I find that these verses, which extol so eloquently the power of friendship, make me both sad and happy at the same time.

Sad, because they remind me that they were the verses given to Evelyn and me by God as we began our relationship so many years ago. Sad, too, because they tell me how much I have lost now my best friend is no longer here to support and encourage me.

But also happy, because I still have so many good friends who have stood by me during these months of bereavement. Happy, too, because I know that here lies one of the main factors in coming through the grief journey – allowing friends to help and sustain us.

Friends are a gift from God, but we must nurture and develop every relationship we have, letting our friends know we love and appreciate them. In turn, we seek to be a loyal and caring friend to them. Thus, the bonds of friendship remain strong and reliable during testing times. To have friends we must be a friend.

Notice that these verses speak about a 'threefold' cord, three strands intertwined. What does this mean? I think it speaks about three people – two friends with Christ between them, holding them together. It is describing spiritual friendship, the strongest form of relationship there can be. It is also a beautiful description of Christian marriage, which has friendship at its heart.

Diversion

A helpful way of dealing with the natural tendency to dwell on negative thoughts following the death of a loved one is to consciously point our mind in another direction. We divert or distract ourselves from the memory of their death by focusing on our memories of their life. In this way we move from remorse over what we have lost, to the happiness of what we enjoyed. Regret is replaced by thankfulness and gratitude.[31]

Another way we can moderate the intensity of our grief is by becoming absorbed in something else. This gives our emotions a rest and is a way of taking time-off from grieving so that we can be strengthened and refreshed to cope with all that we are facing. Lucy Hone says that 'when we ruminate over long stretches of time, covering the same ground over and over again, rumination is not beneficial. Chronic rumination can amplify our negative mood, exacerbating the pain, and rarely leads to an effective solution.'[32] It creates a mental cycle that needs to be broken, and diversion helps to do this and establish healthier thought patterns.

Diversion is not the same as avoidance or denial, but a recognition that it is not healthy to be absorbed all the time with our loss. There are times to confront our loss and feel the pain, but also times to step back and find solace. This is the best way to move forward while dealing with our sadness.

Distraction can take many forms but essentially involves allowing ourselves to be actively engaged in something that absorbs our attention and that we can enjoy. This may include such things as physical exercise (walking, running, swimming, gardening), listening to music, cooking, watching gripping TV programmes or films and reading. We may choose to be with friends or a close companion and talk about things other than our grief. Going out for a meal, shopping, having a coffee and giving ourselves little treats can also help. We may even find that concentrating on work matters for a while may provide a suitable diversion.

However we choose to refocus our minds, we should not feel guilty about enjoying something that gives us respite. We may initially feel some resistance to this, feeling we ought to be grieving all the time, but that is the way to get lost in our grief. Distraction is healthy as long as it is not extreme or persistent and can be a significant part of our recovery.

2 May

Before there was the pandemic in this country there was an epidemic – not of disease, but of loneliness. The months of lockdown have only served to intensify the disconnectedness that many people feel.

In his wonderful book Surrender to Love, *David Benner writes, 'The deepest ache of the soul is the spiritual longing for connection and belonging. No one was created for isolation.'[33] Loneliness at its core is a spiritual matter, a reflection of our disconnection from God, the source of all love.*

During the months of January and February, I experienced an acute sense of loneliness. Having been recently bereaved I found there was a hole in my heart. Although I have many good friends, I still spent hours by myself, a new experience for me after 46 years of marriage. As I ate meal after meal alone in what felt like solitary confinement, I longed for companionship – another person to affirm my existence and worth, another human being to tell me that I matter. I know my experience was not unique. Many others have felt the same way.

Where do we go with our sense of loneliness and isolation?

I realised that God is the source of all love, and that the emptiness I felt inside could only be met by discovering again my identity as his deeply loved child. The God who made me and created me loves me without reservation or condition. To survive I needed to return to the source of my true identity, the foundation of my worth and value. It has not been easy, but I have given my Sunday mornings to the task of reminding myself how deeply I am loved, and how securely I am held by God, the great lover of my soul.

I am on a journey, but I am making progress. Often the loneliness and isolation that we feel is God's wake-up call to bring us back to our heavenly Father.

4 May

I've just taken the car to the garage for some minor issues to be sorted. Normally this was a simple operation. We would take both cars, drop one off, then come back together. Without Evelyn this now becomes a bigger issue, and I am forced to walk back from the garage, this morning a 45-minute hike in blustery and cold conditions. The sense of teamwork, of working together to solve a problem or cope with a situation, is something I miss now she has gone. Even now there are little reminders of the role she played in my life.

5 May

I have been joining an online grief support group facilitation course, led by my good friend Bill Webster. He has a wonderful ministry helping funeral directors care for the needs of their clients, and I have discovered there are many of them who are deeply caring and highly skilled already in helping their clients cope with grief. I am wondering if grief support might be something for me to be involved in later. I see it as being such an important gift to offer people, especially post-pandemic. In grief we meet through our common humanity, and I sense this is a wonderful opportunity for churches to serve their local communities. It is also a great way to bring good out of our pain too.

9 May

I am studying again Benner's <u>Surrender to Love</u> as a way of reminding myself of my true identity as God's deeply loved child. I know that before I can form a new relationship I must be at peace within myself, and that the 'hole' I have often felt – the need for intimacy and connection – must be filled by God first and foremost. Yes, it is God who said, 'It is not good for the man to be alone. I will make a helper suitable for him' (Genesis 2:18). He knows we need human companionship to be fulfilled. Yet no other human *being can fully meet our need for intimacy. Only God can do that, and romantic love must not be confused with divine love.*

I like how Benner brings out the fact that we have been loved by a perfect love (1 John 4:18), a love that invites us to surrender ourselves in response, trusting in the dependable goodness of God. He writes:

> Christian surrender is saying yes to God's Yes! to me. It begins as I experience his wildly enthusiastic, recklessly loving affirmation of me. It grows out of soaking myself in this love so thoroughly that love for God springs up in response. Surrender to his love is the work of his Spirit, making his love ours and his nature ours. This is the core of Christian spiritual transformation.'[34]

13 May

Back home again after a few days away with my sister Jean, which I enjoyed very much. The last time I went away, in September, I found it strange going on holiday without Evelyn. This time it was the coming back that was difficult. But one thing I noticed – I don't feel quite so odd being by myself when I see couples walking together or sitting on benches enjoying the view. I tend to think, 'I hope you appreciate what you have,' and I want to say to them, 'Don't take what you have for granted, however mundane it may seem. One day you may not have it anymore.'

Another thing struck me – how much I miss Evelyn when I am driving. We always helped each other out, checking if it was safe to pull out at junctions and so on. It seems much safer that way, especially as one gets older. Now the responsibility is solely mine.

16 May

Continuing my Sunday morning study with David Benner's <u>Surrender to Love</u>. He devotes a lot of time to the verse which says, 'There is *no fear in love. But perfect love drives out fear, because fear has to do with punishment. The one who fears is not made perfect in love'* (1 John 4:18). *I realise that many of my anxieties about my future are because I am not trusting fully in the love, and the plans, that God has for me. It occurs to me that what matters is not my trying harder to trust God, but my choosing to relax in his trustworthiness. It is not my effort to trust that counts, but the realisation that God is worthy of my trust, that he is utterly reliable and will never let me down even if my trust in him wavers.*

17 May

At the dentist today for the extraction of a wisdom tooth. It should have happened back in March, but I couldn't face it; I seemed to have too much to cope with then. So today we went ahead, but, oh my, it was painful!

19 May

Today work began to remove the old patio at the back of the house and lay a new one. It is the first major change I have made to the house, and I am hoping it works out well. The old patio had been badly laid, and every year has been the bane of my life because of the weeds that grow between the cracks. Hopefully there will be no more getting down on my hands and knees to do weeding.

22 May

The patio is finished, and it looks great. I am so pleased with it. I think Ev would have been as well.

24 May

I drove down today to the beautiful Penhurst Retreat Centre in Sussex. It is a five-hour drive, which is the longest I have driven in the past two years, but I enjoyed the challenge. I have led many retreats here over the years, so it is good to be back, but as I arrived, I had another of those moments when I am aware that Evelyn is no longer here. Normally the first thing I would do on arriving would be to give her a call to let her know all is well. No need to do that now, even though it is an almost instinctive, automatic response for me to call home. And another thing strikes me – I will no longer need to walk up the hill to get a phone signal after the evening meal to give her my daily update. It feels strange to no longer have the connection with home base on my travels.

25 May

The theme of this retreat is 'At home with Jesus', a study of the relationship of Jesus with Martha, Mary and Lazarus as told for us in Luke 10 and John 11. It is a small group of six people, restricted because of coronavirus concerns. We are being led by Amy Boucher Pye, an American author and retreat leader who is married to an Anglican vicar in London. It is good for me to be on the receiving end for a change, and I am happy to be here as a participant. Today I am challenged about the danger of finding meaning through achievement (Martha) and the need to develop intimacy through being with Jesus (Mary).

27 May

Today we studied the story about the death of Lazarus, and it is interesting to see how Jesus helps both Mary and Martha with their grief. Of course, the real question is why did Jesus delay in returning to Bethany, and it makes us think of the delays we have experienced in our own lives and the difficulty of waiting. The big encouragement, though, is the short but significant statement: 'Jesus wept' (John 11:35). It reminds us that he is the man of sorrows and one acquainted with grief (Isaiah 53:3). He knows and understands the pain of loss and meets us in our sorrows. This has been my own experience over the past ten months.

We are encouraged to write our own prayer of lament, and I find the words flow easily. It begins like this:

> *Lord, today I am sad, sad because of all that I have lost when Evelyn died.*
> *I lost my closest friend, my lover, the mother of my children, my rock, my confidante.*
> *I lost the one who loved me, and the one whom I loved in return…*

---

28 May

'Liquid love' is today's title for the retreat, and it is built around the incident where Mary anoints the feet of Jesus with her expensive perfume (John 12:1–3). It is an extravagant act of love, and we wonder if Mary was indeed in love with Jesus. But the challenge for me, as I emerge both from lockdown and my time of mourning, is to offer myself again to the one who is the lover of my soul. The weeks I have spent reading Surrender to Love *come back to me. We give ourselves to God, not because we must, out of duty or compliance, but because we want to, out of love, gratitude and thankfulness for all he has done for us. The words of a hymn by Frances Ridley Havergal (1836–79), which have spoken to me before, seem to sum up my own extravagant response at this moment:*

> *Take my love; my Lord I pour,*
> *At Thy feet its treasure-store.*

As I yield myself again to God for my future, this seems to be a watershed moment for me. It feels like I am leaving the time of mourning behind, and even though I will continue to grieve, I am emerging into a new day where the focus is on the present and the future, not the past – like a butterfly leaving behind the cocoon and, with difficulty, spreading its wings for the first time.

In the afternoon I had some personal time with Amy, which was very beneficial. She describes me as an 'elder statesman', which made me laugh, but hopefully has some truth in it!

29 May
As the retreat comes to an end it is a warm sunny day, and we celebrate Communion outside. We are a disparate group of people, different in so many ways, yet we have enjoyed each other's company and it has done us all good to be with others after the long months of lockdown. Last night we had some great fun talking about our favourite comedians, then discussing what hospitality really means, and then each of us telling a story about meeting someone famous. It was for me all part of the healing process and the adjustment to a new normal. Penhurst is a special place, and the ingredients of beautiful countryside, comfortable surroundings, great food, excellent teaching and warm fellowship make for an enriching few days.

31 May
Facebook reminds me that a year ago today I was admitted to intensive care with Covid-19. What a journey then, and subsequently. Still grateful to God and to all who prayed. Meeting my good friend Cliff for breakfast this morning – celebrating not only this, but our coming through the weeks of lockdown and the birth of his new grandson.

A new season

My beloved spoke and said to me,
   'Arise my darling,
   my beautiful one, come with me.
See! The winter is past;
   the rains are over and gone.

Flowers appear on the earth;
    the season of singing has come,
the cooing of doves
    is heard in our land.
The fig-tree forms its early fruit;
    the blossoming vines spread their fragrance.
Arise, come, my darling;
    my beautiful one, come with me.'
SONG OF SONGS 2:10–13

In the depths of winter my little garden looked barren, forsaken and lifeless for weeks on end. Now that spring is here it is hard to believe the difference. Everything has sprung into life again. The garden once more is verdant and green, awash with colour, bursting with new growth.

The season of mourning can be a long and hard one. For days on end we feel lost and lonely, lacking direction and purpose, simply getting by from one day to the next. It is hard to imagine anything else but a dreary existence now our loved one is gone. But the time of grief is not forever; it is a season, and eventually the life of Christ within us will come bursting through again. Just as winter gives way to spring, mourning will give way to joy.

The beauty of flowers, the joyful singing of birds, the sweet fragrance of blossom, the promise of fruitfulness – these are all signs of a new season, and reminders to us that joy and laughter, fun and happiness, rest and contentment, service and satisfaction will all be ours once again.

The key is to hear and respond to the voice of love: 'Arise my darling, my beautiful one, come with me' (vv. 10, 13). We may have lost the love of our partner but never the love of our Saviour. In his eyes we are still desirable, and his affection and longing for us is undiminished. Our positive response to the call to enter more deeply into his unchanging love is what will bring healing and wholeness to us once again.

Up and down, backwards and forwards, in and out

Contemporary researchers into bereavement sometimes reject the idea of stages in the grief process, preferring to think instead of a flow or movement between confronting our grief, and then avoiding it in order to find respite. This process they describe as oscillation, at one time dealing with our pain and loss for a period, then stepping back from it to deal with other things. This movement is part of the natural or instinctive way we deal with grief. We both face up to it and alternatively turn away from it, in a repeated cycle.

This movement seems more pronounced in the later stages of grief as we begin to rebuild our life and prepare for the future. Initially we are loss-oriented, and the focus is on thinking about our loved one, remembering life as it used to be, reminiscing, shedding our tears, feeling the loss, making our adjustments. Then we become more restoration-oriented, when the focus is on life without the person and we learn to live with the new reality – how to cook or handle finances, living alone and making new friends, making adjustments to the home and decisions about the future, and so on.

Even after many months we may still turn back to the past and discover new ways in which our loss has impacted us. One moment we may feel we are through the worst and recovering nicely; then suddenly we find ourselves feeling lonely, isolated and at a loss about coping. Such is the up and down, backwards and forwards, in and out nature of the grief process.

JUNE 2021

Repositioning

A new adventure

> Not that I have already obtained all this, or have already arrived at my goal, but I press on to take hold of that for which Christ Jesus took hold of me. Brothers and sisters, I do not consider myself yet to have taken hold of it. But one thing I do: forgetting what is behind and straining towards what is ahead, I press on towards the goal to win the prize for which God has called me heavenwards in Christ Jesus.
> PHILIPPIANS 3:12–14

At the start of 2020 I felt God say to me that I still have one more adventure ahead of me. It seemed incongruous at the time because a few weeks later we received the news that Evelyn's condition was terminal, and in some ways our world fell apart. These words have never left me though and now I feel I must respond to them again and believe that God has indeed something ahead for me. He still has a plan for my life, and another season of service awaits.

I am not at all unique in this regard. The apostle Paul carried a strong sense of assurance that God had called him for a specific purpose, and that purpose was not yet finished. This is true of you as well. It may feel as if life has finished, but it has not. There is more ahead of you. God can still make something beautiful of your life and use you in however many years you have left.

Recovering our sense of purpose will give meaning to us post-bereavement. We all need a reason to live, and serving God is one of the highest callings we can have. We do not all serve in the same way. Your way of service will be different to mine, just as your calling is not the same as mine. But you do have a calling and it is important to take hold of it, and to pursue it enthusiastically.

'Forgetting what is behind' does not mean forgetting our loved one but letting go of the life we had before. A new chapter is to be written, and it will be different. Life has provided us with a new opportunity, a chance to start again, and not everyone has that possibility. Let's seize it with both hands and determine to live for God's glory.

Right thinking

Teaching on resilience always emphasises the importance of right thinking. How we interpret what happens to us will largely determine how we respond to those events. If we look at things with a negative, fear-filled mindset, inevitably we run the risk of being overwhelmed by our emotions. Alternatively, if we adopt a more positive and optimistic approach, we will be empowered to cope and pull through. This is certainly true when it comes to grief.

Of course, we need a realistic optimism, not minimising what has happened or denying the difficulties we face. But if we can believe that we will come though the darkness, that the pain will not last forever and that there is still a life worth living, we are more likely to emerge relatively unscathed. This is where faith has a big part to play in our well-being. When we believe that God is in control of events, we can have hope.

Hope is a distinctly Christian attitude that lifts us out of our present circumstances and gives us confidence that better days are ahead of us. Even in the face of death and the loss of some hopes and dreams, new hopes can emerge. Identifying what is still possible will cause optimism to grow again and help us to identify new goals and vision. These may emerge slowly, but emerge they will if we continue to maintain a faith-filled attitude.

Each of us has a battle to fight in our mind. We can surrender to negative thoughts or we can pull back and bring our thoughts under control. We can choose to see that our cup is half full rather than believe it is half empty.

---

2 June
The faithful Nissan Note that has served us so well (The Grey One) is having difficulties, and the Nissan dealer thinks it requires a new gear box, an expensive remedy. Perhaps it is time to sell it? It has such a strong connection to Evelyn, but I can't afford to keep two cars, plus pay out for a hefty repair bill.

---

5 June
Time today with my grandsons, George and Jacob. They are a delight, and it is a joy to spend time with them, although I am usually exhausted afterwards.

---

6 June
The Nissan has gone! Sadness, for many reasons. But Sophie is still here, my beautiful Citroen Cactus.

7 June

Having enjoyed <u>Surrender to Love</u> so much myself, I have invited a group of five friends to study it with me over the next few weeks. Each is a mature believer with a hunger to know God more deeply, and the first session has gone really well. It is amazing how much we learn when we share openly and honestly with one another.

13 June

My first outside preaching engagement, and my first time to church, for about 15 months. Not that I have backslidden, just that due to Covid restrictions my own church has not been able to meet together as yet. This morning I was speaking at a local Anglican church, at both morning services. It was a strange feeling, and I was uncertain how to behave, but I managed well enough in the end. All this while socially distanced, wearing masks and no singing.

15 June

First evening at the T20 Blast cricket over in Leeds, on a wonderfully sunny summer's evening. Good to be with friends and hear the sound again of bat on ball and enjoy the sight of a beautifully manicured cricket field.

16 June

Sitting drinking a coffee in the sunshine at a stunningly beautiful National Trust property. The paper cup says it is made from 'carefully sourced ingredients'. It's a good start to the day and a nice opportunity to practise what I preach about self-care with a little bit of time out for this busy person. Time to breathe, enjoy the sunshine and a good walk with a friend later on. Rest, exercise, friendship – all carefully sourced ingredients of a different kind and essential to our well-being.

17 June

So enjoyed taking part in the 'Self-care for God's servants' seminar online just now, in partnership with Field Partners International. It was a truly global event, which is amazing. I am here in my little office but connecting with people as far apart as Canada, South Africa, Nepal, Singapore and Japan! Truly humbled to share my thoughts with them, and hopefully further equip them for ministry over the long haul.

21 June

I'm just back from a wonderfully refreshing weekend with some friends in Harrogate. Bill and Margaret invited me to visit them in their home some time ago. We enjoyed the beautiful RHS Garden Harlow Carr on Friday, went walking in the Yorkshire Dales on Saturday and then enjoyed fellowship with members of their church, both at the Sunday morning service and at an informal lunch in their beautiful garden afterwards.

Bill and Margaret have the gift of hospitality, and they use it to good effect, opening their home to many in need of rest and refreshment. I felt it was a privilege to be with them, and it has made me marvel at how many people like them God has brought across my path during the past year to strengthen and help me through this time of transition.

I met Bill for the first time at the start of 2020, seemingly by accident. I had been speaking at a seminar in their church, and during the lunch break I happened to sit next to him and we ate our sandwiches together. We seemed to connect deeply and that was when the invitation was first offered. They have kept in touch with me since, during the upheavals of the past 15 months, often re-issuing the invitation to stay with them. I have been invited back anytime, so I must have behaved well. I feel I have made some new friends.

23 June

Another evening at the cricket, another win for Yorkshire, but freezing cold tonight.

27 June

Preaching this morning over in Sheffield. It feels good to have these opportunities and to have the joy of sharing God's word again. How much I have missed all of this.

28 June

Tomorrow would have been Evelyn's 74th birthday, and the first birthday since she died. As time passes I feel her loss not less, but more – not all the time, but in moments of acute awareness that she is no longer here. Just the other day I looked across to her favourite chair and found myself thinking, 'Why aren't you here?' It seems strange to have such a thought after so long, but that is the reality. I have been to the grave this morning to place some flowers and to tidy up. We are still waiting for the gravestone to be ready. Tomorrow Debbie and I will take a trip to York, to be together and remember her mum. York was Evelyn's favourite place, so it seems appropriate.

29 June

Debbie and I had a great day out today, a warm sunny day and York was buzzing with life. We talked, shared our memories, looked at a few photos and videos, and shed a tear. We had a leisurely coffee, did some shopping, had a delicious lunch in a French restaurant, did a bit more shopping, then travelled home. It feels like we celebrated Evelyn's life and enjoyed her presence. To cap it all, England beat Germany 2–0 in the European Championships. Evelyn, with her love and knowledge of football, would have enjoyed that too!

30 June
I have allowed myself to get carried away by too many social activities as lockdown eases. Result? I'm feeling a bit overwhelmed and getting behind with my work. I should have been going to stay overnight with a friend in Birmingham to watch cricket (yes, again!), but decided to bite the bullet and ask if I could be excused. He didn't mind as he wasn't feeling too good himself. It will give me some much-needed breathing space and reduce my internal pressure.

How long does grief last?

> The Israelites grieved for Moses in the plains of Moab thirty days, until the time of weeping and mourning was over.
> DEUTERONOMY 34:8

'How long should I grieve?' is a common question. Most of the advice says that grief takes as long as it takes, that there is no set period, and we should be prepared to allow it to take its course. There is a profound truth in this, of course, but it is not always helpful to the person grieving. 'When will I know my grieving is finished?' is the next question. To this, the almost cryptic reply is, 'You will know in yourself.'

The Jewish people in the Old Testament seem to have had set periods for mourning – sometimes 30 days, as for Moses and for Aaron (Numbers 20:29), but also 70 days (for Joseph, Genesis 50:3). Even today Jewish mourning has identifiable periods. The most intensive mourning is called *shiva* and covers the first seven days, after which normal activities can be resumed. The first month is also significant and *sheloshim* marks the end of this period or religious mourning.

In contemporary British culture there are no hard and fast guidelines, although most people think it important to come through the first year before making too many major decisions or changes. At the same time there are unwritten and unspoken expectations. If you recover too quickly from grief, people are likely to think you didn't care; if you are too slow to adjust, they may think you are stuck in your grief.

Perhaps here the distinction between mourning and grieving is helpful. Mourning, as the outward expression of grief, may be given a time limit, but grief, the emotion we feel inside us, will probably never leave us completely. We can move forward and adapt to life without our loved one, but we never really forget them. Nor should we.

Looking outwards

A time of bereavement is a time for drawing inwards, receiving help and finding comfort, making sense of what has happened to us and allowing ourselves time to heal and recover. These are all self-centred actions, and yet at such a time of loss and pain it is necessary to focus on ourselves for as long as we need until we find our equilibrium again. This is not being selfish, but simply taking care of ourselves. It is normal and natural.

With the passing of time and the recovery of our inner stability, we will find that it is time to reach out again to others. Good relationships are a key in our recovery, and it is right that we learn to receive help and support from others, but healthy relationships are always two-way – a matter of giving and receiving. An early sign of our recovery is when we realise that we have the emotional capacity to feel the pain that others are carrying without thinking of our own, when we can offer support to others in their need without needing help ourselves. This not only helps them, but it helps us also. To forget about our own troubles for a while is a form of therapy in itself. Self-forgetfulness at the right time leads to the road of recovery.

Our experience of bereavement can develop in us a deeper empathy for those who are also grieving. Having received comfort ourselves we may be ideally positioned to offer support to others – we know, for example, what is helpful and what is not. Having received so much ourselves we may feel the desire to give back as an act of gratitude and thankfulness.

Each of us has a story to tell. Without tying them into a similar experience, sharing our grief journey with others can be a great source of help and inspiration. The more honest and humble we can be, the more our story will impact others in a good way.

JULY 2021

Reflecting

God's plans

> 'For I know the plans I have for you,' declares the Lord, 'plans to prosper you and not to harm you, plans to give you hope and a future. Then you will call on me and come and pray to me, and I will listen to you. You will seek me and find me when you seek for me with all your heart.'
> JEREMIAH 29:11–13

Through the prophet Jeremiah God reminds the exiles in Babylon that he has not forgotten them. Their time of separation from the promised land would soon be over and they would return to their homeland. God's plans and purposes continue for them, despite their faithlessness.

There is an abiding truth here, and it is this – that God has a purpose and a plan for each of our lives. During bereavement every aspect of our life is thrown up into the air and we are filled with uncertainty. We may lose sight of the vision God has for us, but God does not. He bides his time to remind us of his purpose and to reveal his plans to us.

His plans are good plans, for he desires to bless us, and submitting to his will can only bring us joy. His plans are gracious plans, for we do not deserve such goodness, but we are blessed nonetheless. We are called to trust in the utterly dependable goodness of God and move forward into the life he has planned for us. We need not think that the best is behind us. There are new surprises just ahead of us!

Our part in this process is to be prayerful, offering ourselves to God again in surrender and availability, seeking to discern (perhaps with the help of others) his will for us going forward. When we do this sincerely, with openness and humility, he will speak and direct our paths. We will discover what we already knew – that all his paths are good and right.

Changed by grief

There is no doubt that the experience of grief can change us significantly, and for the better if we work with the process. Positive change is not a given. It depends on how well we grieve and how open we are to be changed by our experience, but grief can provide us with a doorway to growth.

Hopefully we become *deeper* people, freed from the shallowness associated with a comfortable life. Our world has been shaken to the core and, having lost the person who probably meant most to us in the whole world, we have been forced to plumb the depths mentally, emotionally and spiritually. We know what suffering is, and we will never be the same.

Because we have had such an experience and survived, we are now *stronger* people. We have had to find ways to cope with our loss, to get through many dark and difficult days. We have confronted loneliness, tasted despair, faced the grave. The icy winds of adversity have blown over our lives, but we have come through. We have learned to dig deep within ourselves to discover inner resources, to turn in prayer to God with a plaintive cry for help, to depend on friends and family for succour and comfort. If we can get through this, we can get through most things. We have become resilient.

Having been on the receiving end of so much kindness from others, perhaps our hearts have been softened and we are now *kinder* people. Our neediness has attuned us to the needs of others, and our sense of gratitude forged a new generosity of spirit within us. We can no longer be content with a self-centred life that grasps and consumes. We have been liberated to give and to care.

We emerge from the tribulation of our loss a little humbler and certainly a degree *wiser*. We have grown up inside, become more mature. We realise that we don't understand everything and certainly can't control everything, which is the beginning of wisdom. We now know for sure that life is best lived in harmony with God and in dependence upon his grace. We are aware that life is frail, fragile and finite. We appreciate we must value our relationships and cherish our friendships and take nothing or no one for granted. We treat each day as a gift, thank God for the gift of life and seek to live with gratitude and joy.

---

4 July
Violently sick during the night and today lacking in energy. Definitely missing Evelyn's nursing skills and reassuring presence. Is it my cooking?

---

5 July
Recorded an interview today for UCB, a Christian radio station, about my book <u>Deep Calls to Deep</u>*, which is based on the book of Psalms and has just been re-issued. It looks at some of the psalms where the writer cries to God 'out of the depths' and uses them to*

show how God is at work in us even in the hard places of life. It also has six amazing testimonies of people who heard God's invitation to go deeper with him during their times of hardship and affliction, to which I can now add my own testimony.

6 July

Evelyn loved her garden and her greenhouse, and I have struggled to keep on top of things by myself, but nature is marvellous and somehow despite me the plants and shrubs manage to blossom and flower. The very cycle of growth and the regularity of the seasons visually reminds me of her. Today, for example, the agapanthus that we brought from a holiday in Madeira is in bud, and the lily from which I took a cutting to place on her coffin is ready to bloom again, right on cue.

8 July

I find myself in reflective mood as I begin to look back over the past twelve months. What am I learning from my grief journey? Here are a few standouts lessons:

1 *Grief takes longer than we think to work itself through, and it can't be rushed. It is a journey, and we must travel slowly.*

2 *When we lose our partner, we lose not only the person we loved, but the person who loved us. This second loss is the hardest to bear and leaves a hole in the heart, which means for a while we are very vulnerable when it comes to relationships.*

3 *We will need to rediscover our identity as God's deeply loved child in this season of our life, as if we had never known it before.*

4 God can be trusted to help us rebuild our life, but trust may not come easily. It is better to focus on God's trustworthiness than on our ability to trust, which may be shaky.

5 Our experience of grief and our response to loss is unique and personal, so we don't compare our journey to that of others. We can learn from others, but our pathway is ours alone.

9 July

Here is a second list of things I am learning, with the emphasis on learning, as it is a continuing experience. They are in no particular order:

6 Good friends can make the journey so much easier.
   Be prepared to ask for help; be ready to receive help.

7 We will be ambushed by grief. You can anticipate many things, but some things will take us by surprise, especially the little things.

8 The loss of a spouse will leave us feeling very lonely, even when we are surrounded by family and friends. This is not a weakness, just a sign of what we have lost – deep companionship.

9 Loneliness is not a mental illness, just a natural response to being bereaved, and it will get better.

10 Moving forward is not a sign that we didn't care, but that there is still a life to be lived and not wasted.

10 July

A few more reflections. Hopefully you are not bored yet!

11 It helps to talk about our loss and the person we have lost. Sharing our story helps us to put things together in our mind and is healing in itself. We can speak about our loved one by name, often and openly.

12 Don't be afraid of pain, and don't anaesthetise it or avoid it – acknowledge it, face it, and we will heal more quickly.

13 Crying is normal, even for men, and healing in itself. Don't be afraid of this even in public.

14 It will surprise us who draws near to us in our grief, and who steps away. Appreciate those who come closer, without judging those who hold back – they will have their own good reasons.

15 Not everything people say to us about grief and how we should respond to it will be helpful. We can decide for ourselves what is important for us.

---

11 July

A final posting about the lessons I have been learning over the past year:

16 Grief may expose some of our weaknesses and inner faultlines, but don't be afraid of this – learning more about ourselves is a gift that comes with grieving.

17 No one grieves perfectly. We will make mistakes, bad choices and errors of judgement. This is normal – we can forgive ourselves; we are human.

18 Hope will rise again within us. The human spirit, in combination with God's grace, has its own remarkable resilience and we will bounce back.

19 Don't be afraid to live again. God has a good purpose for us, and a plan for our life.

20 Your faith is an asset, not a liability. When we are tempted to be angry with God, or wonder where he is, remember that he is the source of our strength and an ever-present help in time of need. Lean on him, ask for his help.

21 We have a part to play in our grief journey, so we must not be passive and allow it to overwhelm us. We must do what we can to rebuild our life.

12 July

Today I am joining a small group of friends in the beautiful Peak District in Derbyshire for what we have called 'A little summer get-together'. Holidays can be difficult when you are by yourself, so it is nice to be part of a group. I did not realise though when my friend Jenny and I made plans to organise a group holiday that it would coincide with the anniversary of Evelyn's death. I wonder how I will feel tomorrow?

13 July

Glad to say I have not felt too upset today, I think because Debbie and I marked Evelyn's birthday so well just two weeks ago. I had some time to myself first thing, and then at the end of the day. In between I was glad of the company and the diversion of a trip to Hardwick Hall.

16 July

The week has been a great success, better than we could have hoped for – a wonderful week of friendship and fellowship, walking and talking, coffee and cake, worship and teaching, fun and laughter. It's wonderful to have an idea to do something, to be given the faith to go for it, to see it come about and then for it to exceed expectations.

17 July

Back home now and facing the expected blip of loneliness after being with people all week. Coming back to an empty house with no one to talk to about my adventures is not easy, but it has not been as hard as I expected, an indicator that I have made progress on my grief journey. I think this is a good sign. I am adjusting to the new reality.

Just before I went away I received a review copy of Penelope Swithinbank's excellent book on grief called <u>Scent of Water</u>. I didn't understand the title at first, until I read on one of the early pages that this expression is taken from the Bible: 'There is hope for a tree: if it is cut down, it will sprout again... at the scent of water it will bud and put forth shoots like a plant' (Job 14:7, 9).

I have to say I was unfamiliar with this reference, but when I read it tears filled my eyes at the realisation that this has been exactly my experience. I was like a tree that had been cut down, and hope was gone, and yet, by God's grace, I am coming back to life again. The comfort of God has flowed towards me, and I have sensed again his love for me – the scent of water – and my soul has responded. I feel his life within me sprouting once again.

Epilogue

To sit and write these words has been such a privilege, and so cathartic for me. To go over in detail the events of the past year has helped me see how far I have come and reminded me of all that has happened during that time. Emotions have risen to the surface again as memories have been triggered, some happy, some sad, but each a valid part of this journey I have so unwillingly taken. I can't imagine that I will ever go back to those dark days of January and February, which is a relief. I wonder now how I came through such times, but I did, and here I am, still standing (by God's grace).

I have battled through a continuing sense of loss, the feeling that something vital is missing, and struggled with times of uncertainty, self-doubt and deep concerns about my future. There have been so many new things to learn – how to cook, do the washing and ironing, the shopping and tending the garden. It has been such a steep learning curve with so much new information to try to absorb. And loneliness – what can ever prepare one for that?

I am fully aware that my grief journey is far from over, but a significant milestone has been reached. The first year has passed. I have made mistakes along the way and been impatient, wanting to rush through this passage in my life. I am relieved to know that no one's grief journey is perfect. But I have also been brave and persevered, and I celebrate that. Not that I can claim credit. Many prayers have been offered on my behalf, many friends have supported me along the way and, of course, my heavenly Father has never for a moment forsaken me.

Now the journey continues, but where to? What will this new normal look like as things settle down again? I have no idea, so I must put my hand in the hand of God and trust that he who has brought me safely this far will continue to lead and guide me. My future is safe with him.

Notes

1 Bill Webster, *When Someone You Care About Dies* (Centre for the Grief Journey, 2015), p. 4.
2 Webster, *When Someone You Care About Dies*, p. 7.
3 The photo, taken by David Tanner, is the basis for the cover of this book. Why not ponder it for yourself?
4 Webster, *When Someone You Care About Dies*, p. 3.
5 Webster, *When Someone You Care About Dies*, p. 17.
6 Delia Smith, *Delia's How to Cook: Book one* (BBC Books, 1998), p. 11.
7 *Lectio 365* is a free daily devotional from 24-7 Prayer International which I have listened to regularly during the past year when my concentration for reading has been lacking. For more about Henri Nouwen, see **henrinouwen.org**.
8 Bev Shepherd, 'Navigating Transition' email, London Institute of Contemporary Christianity, Day 8, 2020
9 Marcelo Bielsa, *Daily Mail*, Saturday 3 October 2020.
10 GriefShare is a video-based grief support programme from Church Initiative, a ministry from the USA that creates and publishes video-based curriculums to help churches minister to people experiencing life crises. See **griefshare.org**.
11 Tony Horsfall, *Finding Refuge: Love in a time of lockdown* (Charis Training, 2020), p. 1.
12 Elisabeth Kübler-Ross and David Kessler, *On Grief and Grieving: Finding the meaning of grief through the five stages of loss* (Simon and Schuster, 2005).
13 Ian Jennings, *What is Life without My Love? A practical guide to coping with the loss of a loved one* (2020), p. 21.
14 Lois Tonkin, 'Growing around grief – another way of looking at grief and recovery', *Bereavement Care*, 15:1 (1996), p. 10.
15 Julia Samuel, *Grief Works: Stories of life, death and surviving* (Penguin Life, 2017), pp. 41–50.

16 'Epiphany', *Lectio 365* devotional app by 24-7 Prayer, 6 January 2021, **24-7prayer.com/lectio365**. Used by permission.
17 'Undeserved mercy', *Lectio 365* devotional app by 24-7 Prayer, 21 January 2021, **24-7prayer.com/lectio365**. Used by permission.
18 'Rest in the blessing', *Lectio 365* devotional app by 24-7 Prayer, 24 January 2021, **24-7prayer.com/lectio365**. Used by permission.
19 Tony Horsfall, *Deep Calls to Deep: Spiritual formation in the hard places of life* (BRF, 2021).
20 Eugene Peterson, *The Message of David* (Marshall Pickering, 1997), p. 105.
21 Kübler-Ross and Kessler, *On Grief and Grieving*, p. 81.
22 Richard Littledale, *Postcards from the Land of Grief: Comfort for the journey through loss towards hope* (Authentic, 2019).
23 Jeff Manion, *The Land Between: Finding God in difficult transitions* (Zondervan, 2010), p. 19.
24 'Valentine's Day blessing', *Lectio 365* devotional app by 24-7 Prayer, 14 February 2021, **24-7prayer.com/lectio365**. Used by permission.
25 Sharon Garlough Brown, *Sensible Shoes: A story about the spiritual journey* (IVP, 2013).
26 'Stupid ain't stupid', *Lectio 365* devotional app by 24-7 Prayer, 5 March 2021, **24-7prayer.com/lectio365**. Used by permission.
27 David Atkinson, *The Message of Ruth: Wings of refuge* (IVP, 1983), p. 122.
28 Lucy Hone, *Resilient Grieving: Finding strength and embracing life after a loss that changes everything* (The Experiment, 2017). This book confirmed to me that my approach to grieving after the first six months, and being more proactive than passive, was on the right lines. Many of my reflections on grieving from this point onwards in the book have been influenced by Hone's approach.
29 'Haven't you got any fish?', *Lectio 365* devotional app by 24-7 Prayer, 8 April 2021, **24-7prayer.com/lectio365**. Used by permission.
30 Hone, *Resilient Grieving*, ch. 7.
31 Hone, *Resilient Grieving*, ch. 8.
32 Hone, *Resilient Grieving*, p. 98.
33 David G. Benner, *Surrender to Love: Discovering the heart of Christian spirituality* (IVP, 2003), p. 12.
34 Benner, *Surrender to Love*, p. 66.

Further reading

David Benner, *Surrender to Love: Discovering the heart of Christian spirituality* (IVP, 2003).

John R. Claypool, *Tracks of a Fellow Struggler: Living and growing through grief* (Morehouse Publishing, 1974).

Malcolm Duncan, *Good Grief: Living with sorrow and loss* (Monarch, 2020).

Tony Horsfall, *Finding Refuge: Love in a time of lockdown* (Charis Training, 2020).

Tony Horsfall and Debbie Hawker, *Resilience in Life and Faith: Finding your strength in God* (BRF, 2019).

Lucy Hone, *Resilient Grieving: Finding strength and embracing life after a loss that changes everything* (The Experiment, 2017).

Ian Jennings, *By a Departing Light: Growing through grief* (Self-published, 2018).

Ian Jennings, *What Is Life Without My Love? A practical guide to coping with the loss of a loved one* (Self-published, 2020).

Robert W. Kelleman, *God's Healing for Life's Losses: How to find your hope when you're hurting* (BMH Books, 2010).

David Kessler, *Finding Meaning: The sixth stage of grief* (Rider, 2019).

Allen Klein, *Embracing Life after Loss: A gentle guide for growing through grief* (Mango Publishing, 2019).

Elisabeth Kübler-Ross and David Kessler, *On Grief and Grieving: Finding the meaning of grief thorugh the five stages of loss* (Simon and Schuster, 2005).

C.S. Lewis, *A Grief Observed* (Faber and Faber, 2013).

Richard Littledale, *Postcards from the Land of Grief: Comfort for the journey through loss towards hope* (Authentic, 2019).

Jeff Manion, *The Land Between: Finding God in difficult transitions* (Zondervan, 2010).

Jennifer Rees-Larcombe, *Beauty from Ashes: Readings for times of loss* (BRF, 2010).

Julia Samuels, *Grief Works: Stories of life, death and surviving* (Penguin Life, 2017).

Jerry Sittser, *A Grace Disguised: How the soul grows through loss* (Zondervan, 1995).

Penelope Swithinbank, *Scent of Water: Words of comfort in times of grief* (Sarah Grace, 2021).

Bill Webster, *Help Me If You Can: Coping with life-threatening situations* (The Centre for the Grief Journey, 2003).

Bill Webster, *When Someone You Care About Dies* (The Centre for the Grief Journey, 2015).

Bill Webster, *Now What? Finding your way after a loss* (The Centre for the Grief Journey, 2003).

Granger E. Westberg, *Good Grief* (SPCK, 2011).

Helpful resources and courses

Ataloss	**ataloss.org**
The Bereavement Journey	**thebereavementjourney.org**
Care for the Family	**careforthefamily.org.uk**
Centre for the Grief Journey	**griefjourney.com**
Cruse Bereavement Care	**cruse.org.uk**
GriefShare	**griefshare.org**
Living with Loss	**livingwithloss555742461.wordpress.com**
Marie Curie	**mariecurie.org.uk**
Teardrop	**teardropgrief.co.uk**
What's Your Grief	**whatsyourgrief.com**
Association of Christian Counsellors	**acc-uk.org**